Chellammal's Journal

Chellammal's Journal:

A Woman's Memoir of a Joint Family in Early Twentieth-Century India

Translated from the Tamil by
Kanchana Viswanathan

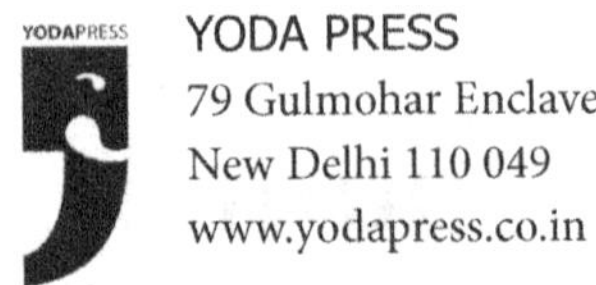
YODA PRESS
79 Gulmohar Enclave
New Delhi 110 049
www.yodapress.co.in

ISBN 978-93-82579-31-1

Editors in charge: Tanya Singh and Chitraksh Ashray
Typeset in Adobe Caslon Pro, 11/14.4
By MSourcing
Published by Arpita Das for YODA PRESS

To Amma and Appa
And my parents Akka and Athimber
…for their nurture and unconditional love, and for
encouraging me to fly high….

Contents

Foreword

This foreword is to tell you about the Chellammal I knew—my mother as I understood her. I, Kanchana, was my mother's youngest child and daughter. Amma was almost 40 when I was born. Most of the incidents mentioned in her memoir happened before my birth.

Chellammal was born in 1920 in Karamanai, Trivandrum. She was married at the age of 12 to Chidambarakrishnan and hence had to stop going to school after eighth standard. She joined her husband and in-laws' family in Vadiveeswaram, Nagercoil and lived in the same house for more than 80 years until she passed away in January 2016 at the age of 95. She had her first child at 16.

After her husband died in 1995, leaving all his property and savings to her, she was financially comfortable, liked her solitude and independence and chose to live alone in the large house. As a person, Chellammal was soft-spoken and not overly emotional; she was averse to melodrama. When she was not busy with household chores, she was a voracious reader and read Tamil magazines and books. She also attempted to write Tamil novels. Later, she focused on writing her memoirs and describing events in her life interspersed with her social commentary on the plight of women. Many of her life experiences are poignantly and powerfully described in her memoirs. She prided herself on being an independent thinker and regretted the fact that her intellect was not recognized or appreciated by her peers and her family.

Chellammal was not a religious person. She performed her prayers and *pujai* because of a sense of duty but rarely visited the local temple or participated in any rituals. She also made it a point to state repeatedly, and publicly, that she did not believe in superstitions. Chellammal sang well but not very often. However, she had a keen ear for Carnatic music and was an expert at identifying *raga*s. She had an insatiable curiosity to learn and know more about languages, peoples and customs. She treated everyone with respect and kindness, irrespective of their caste or creed. Her social consciousness was underscored by the fact that she made arrangements on her own with the local hospital to donate her eyes; her bequest was carried out soon after her passing in 2016.

Chellammal was well-travelled, mostly during the latter part of her life. She visited places all over India, including Kashmir, and went to the United States of America (USA) three times.

Amma's life can be divided into two parts: her life in the joint family before she turned 40 and her more independent later years. Four of us lived in the home that I was born and raised in, my parents, my brother Kumar—Amma's favourite son, seven years older than me—and myself. My older sister Shobha (22 years older than me) and my oldest brother Neelakantan (20 years older than me) both lived elsewhere by the time I was born; first when they went to college and later when they got married. Amma has mentioned in these memoirs that the older children, growing up in a joint family, did not bond with her as their mother. My siblings later agreed that this perception was true to some extent.

I was born two years after the demise of my paternal grandfather (my mother's father-in-law and her neme-sis). I think the pregnancy was unexpected. When I asked Amma about it, she replied, "I had you because I wanted a child." I always felt that she said that to make me feel wanted.

My sister Shobha came back from her college hostel to help Amma when I was a new born. She would later adopt me. Apparently, I cried a lot during the night and both she and Amma would take turns to rock me in the cradle. On one such occasion, Amma remarked, "Seems like the father-in-law has been born again—he just can-not let me be in peace." Shobha Akka would relate this incident to me and laugh.

After the demise of my grandfather, his surviving second wife, my father's stepmother, whom everyone ad-dressed as Chithi, left for Chennai to live with her son. By then I think Chithi's mother Paatti had passed away and my father, Chidambarakrishnan, had become a fa-mous and successful lawyer in Nagercoil. There were no financial problems in our household when I was growing up. We had a car and a driver. Apart from us, at that time, there was only one other household on our street with a car. We regularly went to the movies as a family. We also went to Carnatic music concerts. We often drove to

Kanyakumari (a 12 km drive) and made several long road trips to cities (Chennai and Cochin) and places of pilgrimage (Pazhani and Guruvayur).

Amma's sister-in-law and my aunt (Athai), Seethai, lived on the next street. She would visit us often and was always very affectionate towards me. I have heard that she was the one who raised my older sister Shobha and was close to her. When she spoke about Shobha, she would affectionately refer to her as "daughter". Her interactions with my mother also seemed very cordial. At festival times, when special snacks and delicacies like *murukku, poli, thattai* or *vadaam* needed to be made, Amma would always ask Seethai for help. I have gone many times to my aunt's house on the next street to deliver the message requesting help. Seethai was proficient in making snacks and in particular, she made perfect *murukku* rings, which are difficult to make. However, although on the surface Amma was always pleasant to Seethai, I do not think she truly forgave her for the past.

I have never seen Amma lose her temper, talk loudly or cry a lot. She didn't like participating in gossip or engaging with women whom she felt were ill-informed and superstitious. Amma treated the servants with dignity. She had a great interest in music and frequently sang M.S. Subbulakshmi's famous Mira *bhajans* and Sakuntala songs. She had a good voice and could hold a tune, having a good knowledge of Carnatic music. She was the person Appa always consulted when he had a question about a *ragam* or scale.

Amma seemed to have some faith in God, but never recited verses from religious texts like most other women in our neighbourhood did as part of their daily rituals. Frequently she would proclaim, "I do not have superstitions like these other women." However, she would follow the custom of taking a bath after an eclipse to ward off evil. When questioned about this inconsistent behaviour, she would say, "These stupid neighbours would blame me otherwise." My brother Kumar and I never completely believed her explanation, and we would often argue with her.

Amma wrote these memoirs and revised them multiple times over many years. As children, Kumar and I have seen her trying to hide her writings. That happened when I was seven. When she finally gave me the memoirs in 1996, I was 37 years old.

Amma never discussed the incidents of her youth with me. Once in a while she would say, "There is no limit to what I endured in this house. I will never forget those days," to which Appa would ask rhetorically, "What is to be gained by not forgetting?" Many a time, Amma expressed her desire to move out of our village home in Vadiveeswaram to a nicer place on the outskirts (Ramavarmapuram) of Nagercoil. Invariably, Appa would evade the request and would say, "No place is as convenient as Vadiveeswaram."

Even after prosperity came, she did not buy much in the way of clothes or jewellery for herself. She would only buy cheap clothing for me. Every summer, during the school holidays, the three of us, Amma, Appa and myself (Kumar was away attending college in Chennai and later left for postgraduate studies in America) would go to visit Shobha Akka at her place (Chennai, Bombay and Delhi at different times) for one to two months. As soon as we would arrive, Akka would take me shopping to get new clothes. She would say that whatever Amma had bought for me was of very poor quality. Along with Akka and brother-in-law Raj (later my legal father), we visited many tourist places and landmarks all over India—the Taj Mahal in Agra, Kashmir, Rishikesh, Kodaikanal and many more. Amma was more interested in the people in the different states we travelled to and their myriad languages and customs, than in seeing the sites. She also tried to learn and speak Hindi.

Kumar left for America in the mid-seventies. Amma was not at all happy about his going so far away. Then Kumar married an American. He informed us about his wedding through a letter, hurting Amma but she did not cry. Ultimately, Amma and Appa visited the US in 1986. They spent some time in Kumar's place in Boston. Getting restless, Appa returned to India in one month and never visited the US again. Appa was very well-read and had a deep knowledge of the English language. We had an extensive library of English books at our home. However, he was not very comfortable or familiar with the English spoken in America, and hence apparently would not or could not participate in conversations. At one of the parties at Kumar's place, a friend of his from Kerala had enquired of Kumar in Malayalam, "Does he (your father) know English?" Amma would relate this incident to others and laugh. While in Boston, Amma cooked Kumar's favourite dishes. Once she made *kozhakattai*, the classic steamed rice dumplings. Kumar's American wife, tasting it for the first time, liked it very much and ate it with a can of tuna. Amma described this in great detail and exclaimed, "I could not take it! How can anyone eat such wonderful and delicious *kozhakattai* with fish?" She said this light-heartedly and did not seem too upset.

After visiting Kumar in Boston, Amma came to California to visit me. I was newly married then. We took her to a casino in Reno. She won $50 with a 25-cent bet placed in the slot machine and enjoyed the sound of the shower of coins falling out of the machine. We also took her to a late-night adult show. The women dancers wore skimpy clothes and Amma said, somewhat admiringly, "They are half-naked but have such good figures—like beautifully sculpted statues—and so it does not appear anywhere near as vulgar as it does in some of our Indian movies."

We visited Hearst Castle, a fairy-tale castle built by a newspaper magnate. We had to buy relatively expensive tickets to see the place. My mother commented, "Why would anyone pay money to see this place? In India, we have so many more beautiful palaces. It seems like it doesn't take much to get the Americans to come out in large numbers and pay."

Amma made two more trips to America, in 1990 and again in 1996, after Appa passed away. While in the US, Amma had no desire to go sightseeing. If we went shopping in a mall, she was more than happy and content to sit on a bench and watch people and regale us with her sharp and witty observations. Once we took her to a western classical music concert with a full orchestra. She complained it was too noisy.

It was when Amma visited in 1996 that she gave me the manuscript of her memoirs. I have always wondered why she chose (among the four siblings) to give it to me.

She probably felt that I would be the person most likely to make an effort to get her story out to others. After I first read it, I asked her, "Why have you not written about the good days (the ones I witnessed as I was growing up)?" She did not give me a straight answer. When I pointed out that, "The difficulties you faced in the joint family were faced by many women at that time," she did not like that and was probably hurt.

She merely replied, "What I went through was immense. How could any of you understand?"

The final draft given to me is dated 1993. The prose is intense and powerful. She has started with a description of her early life, most of which was spent in a joint family after she was married at the age of 12. Chellammal shares her own life experiences about the myriad facets of the complex relationships in the family—love, beauty, anger, hate, disappointment—and the sheer drudgery of a wife and mother's role in early twentieth-century South India. She also comments on them with great sensitivity and perception, elevating the writing. The reader can feel the intensity and depth of the experiences with the words drawing you in, asking you to participate and understand.

These memoirs not only express a woman's pain, anguish and agony, they also give voice to the voiceless—all the young girls, wives and widows—for whom life was so difficult, so full of disappointment and disrespect, all who suffered in silence. In her narrative, she has interspersed descriptions of memorable events in her life with her reflections on the plight of women, both in the context of her situation and in general. I felt that the content is still very relevant to women all over the world, whose aspirations and potential are ignored and whose needs are suppressed because of societal, religious and political pressures. (Having lived and worked as a physician in the US for many decades, I have noticed this first-hand, time and time again.) The challenges faced by women are universal and still very serious, more than a century after my mother's early life experiences.

Chellammal seems to have deliberately repeated her views on social issues that affected her deeply, in different sections of the manuscript. She comes back several times in her narrative to the theme of the mistreatment of widows by the orthodox Hindu society that she was part of in her younger days, where young widows were forced to withdraw from society and live a painful existence in the shadows. Her disdain for this practice seems to have been shaped and reinforced by her witnessing the plight of her older sister, who was widowed at a very young age. Amma saw many powerful women in her own family: her widowed grandmother who continued to take care of her body by oiling it, bathing with Pears soap and who was financially independent, and her own mother, who ran the house wisely. Many others broke norms in her family and the society, even before her time, and yet she keeps going back to widows and the indignities they suffered because the images of her mother and her sister are indelibly etched on her mind. The popular TV serials, which she seems to have been in the habit of watching, also harped on the politics of the family, conflating the past and the present in a way that erased all conflicts, changes and resistance. In her writing, she refers to these serials at various times to bring force to her argument.

A unique and very interesting feature of my mother's early life experience is the influence of the teachings of the great nineteenth-century Tamil saint and mystic, Vallalar (Ramalinga Swamigal), who shapted her thoughts and opinions. Her grandfather, the patriarch of her family, was an active devotee of Vallalar and a practitioner of his philosophy. In these memoirs, she has emphasized that her family did not believe in the traditions of *shastra*s or superstitions. She learned from her grandfather about Vallalar's teachings and Vallalar preached that god should be worshipped in the abstract, as a bright glorious light. His teachings emphasized compassion for all living creatures and he treated everyone as equal, regardless of caste or religion.

In retrospect, I feel that we did not adequately acknowledge my mother's intelligence and potential, and the initiative she took on her own to participate in forward-thinking groups. I remember that when I was about six years old, she became a member of what was then a unique and unusual institution in Nagercoil for the times, a women's club. I went with her to some meetings, which must have left a deep impression on me. My recollection is that these were working women, from the Christian part of town, more educated but still very respectful towards my mother.

A few words about Appa. He was very well respected by his family and the people in the town. He rarely showed anger and said that anger was a sign of weakness. Appa would buy a new car every two years. He also spent money on books but did not buy anything else. He was very hardworking and began his workday at 6 a.m. every day and did not stop till 11 p.m. Besides reading to prepare his legal case briefs, he read a great variety of English books, especially fiction, science and philosophy. Many times, he would read and share interesting quotes with me. He was brilliant in Maths. In his own way, he showed love and respect towards my Amma. We went together as a family to movies and concerts and when he had questions about music, he regarded Amma as the ultimate authority. He worked till he turned 80, and then he had to slow down due to illness. He died in 1995 at the age of 82 and he wrote a simple will leaving all his assets to his wife so that she always remained financially independent.

When I was young, we had 24-hour clean running water from the taps in Vadiveeswaram. That changed and ultimately there was water only every three days. To store water, Appa constructed a large tank in the courtyard in the centre of the house. Amma felt it looked ugly. His justification was that it was the cheapest option. After his demise, she had that tank removed and had an underground sump tank built. She always wanted to build an out house, as an annexe to the main house, and rent it out. She went ahead and did that too. The lady (Mahalaxmi) who rented the place cooked and ate fish. Amma was a pure vegetarian but had no problem with this. She liked Mahalaxmi, who she thought was vibrant and independent. Mahalaxmi had once won a local municipal election as a representative of Dravida Munnetra Kazhagam (DMK). Mahalaxmi had also adopted and raised an abandoned child, despite having her children to take care of. Towards the end, when Amma was ill, Mahalaxmi was a devoted caregiver.

After Appa's passing in 1995, Amma lived alone in that large house. She wanted it that way. Others were worried but she enjoyed the solitude. Five years later, the older son Neelakantan moved in from Gujarat after his retirement. Neelakantan had lost his wife to cancer many years ago. Relatives felt he would be good company and support for his mother, but initially, she was not happy to give up her independence. However, she got used to it as time passed. By the time she turned 90 and dementia set in, she could not have continued to stay in that house without his help and support. She died peacefully at home in 2016 at the age of 96.

She did not write a will. Once when I brought up the topic (no one else seemed to want to address the subject), she evaded the question. She said something like, "I know what I should do."

As she slowly faded away and dementia took its toll, I reread her memoirs and decided to translate them to English so that others could also feel the power of her words that I only then realized. Even as I was translating what I thought was her complete memoirs, we recently found, quite by accident, another 62 pages of reminiscences shoved under the mattress of the bed that Chellammal slept in during her final years. These reminiscences also go back and forth in time and are not chronological. Perhaps these new notes (presumably written at a later stage in her life) will shed some light on her thoughts and opinions as she grew older and was alone in the Vadiveeswaram house after all the children had grown up, married and moved away. It is also possible that she felt that the longer notes would benefit from these pages found later which talk much more about her inner conflicts in her marital home, her travels and importantly, her intimate conversations with her husband where she expresses her frustrations and even suggests that he should find her a house where she can live on her own with her youngest child, that he could visit her there and also give her half of his income every month.

At the end of the note found later, she goes back to an incident before her father-in-law's death which portrays her sister-in-law, Seethai, in a bad light. But for some strange reason, she does not complete the last word. It is broken and left incomplete. Considering how detailed her reminiscences are, why did she abruptly stop at this point and write only three letters of that word? Did the doorbell ring? Was the milk boiling over? Did she have to urgently attend to something else? Or did she feel pain and feel physically ill? One will never know. The pages of this supplementary note are smeared with water stains that run over the words. Looking at them one wonders, are they teardrop stains? Did she cry while writing the note, alone in that house in Vadiveeswaram?

Since the point of this supplementary note was her conversation with her husband, Chidambaram and everything else, in a way, revolves around that, I have given it the title "An Open Conversation with Chidambaram" and have presented it the way it was written.

I wish I had shown more empathy towards her and the unrealized ambitions of her youth. I deeply regret never having praised her intellect and writing abilities. By sharing her words and thoughts with a wider audience, I hope to make amends and keep her memories eternal.

This foreword would not be complete without expressing my thanks to Rama Viswanathan, my husband, who helped me put the manuscript together in a certain order, and my family that took a keen interest in my translation efforts. My thanks are also due to Kannan Sundaram who published the original Tamil version through his publishing house Kalachuvadu. The original handwritten memoirs along with the photographs are archived in SPARROW (Sound & Picture Archives for Research on Women) located in Mumbai which is headed by Dr C.S. Lakshmi who writes under the pseudonym, Ambai, in Tamil. I am grateful to her for editing the Tamil version for publication and also for her advice and suggestions in my endeavour to translate Chellammal's memoirs to English. Finally, I wish to acknowledge my deep gratitude to Tanya Singh, Editor and Development Manager at Yoda Press, for her expert guidance in bringing to fruition the publication of this translation.

Kanchana Viswanathan, M.D., F.A.C.E.

Long Beach, California

October 23, 2021

****

Notes on Translation
and Background Information

These memoirs were written—and extensively rewritten—in Tamil by Chellammal, with a final revision by her in 1993 at the age of 73. In the English translation, we have attempted to maintain the tone and the informal, conversational yet incisive style of the original manuscript. We have also tried to convey this unique tone, basically a written version of the typical Tamil "conversation" where all remarks are made rapid-fire and people rarely pause to explicitly listen to or acknowledge the other person. To retain Chellammal's original flow of thoughts, we have not tampered with the manuscript in any way or rearranged it in any manner, except for breaking it into chapters and making some necessary paragraph breaks. Chellammal easily and abruptly jumps from one story to another in her narration. In our chapterization of her narration, which has no breaks as such, we have also retained the abrupt manner in which she begins and ends certain portions, often digressing and returning to what she was saying initially.

Nagercoil is a bustling town situated in the southernmost part of India, close to Kanyakumari, the Cape where the Bay of Bengal, Indian Ocean and the Arabian Sea meet. It is also very close to the border between the states of Tamil Nadu and Kerala, leading to a unique culture where most of the residents are bilingual and can speak/understand both Tamil and Malayalam. Most of the events narrated happened in Vadiveeswaram village, a neighbourhood of Nagercoil.

***

People

Chellammal

Chidambaram aka Chidambarakrishnan (husband)

Chattai aka Neelakantan (father-in-law) who was addressed and referred to as Anna.

Chithi (husband's stepmother)

Paatti (Chithi's mother or Chellammal's grandmother, depending on context).

Seethai (husband's elder sister)

Pappa (husband's younger sister)

Vaidyanathan (husband's younger brother)

Thanu, Neelakantan and Ganapathi (husband's stepbrothers)

Manni aka Lakshmi (Chellammal's mother). Many girls in South India are named after the Goddess Lakshmi and so this name is also encountered in other contexts in the narrative.

Appa (Chellammal's father), who was addressed and referred to as Anna.

Meena (Chellammal's elder sister)

Chellammal's Children: Shobha aka Subbalaxmi (eldest), Neelakantan, Kumar and Kanchana.

Places

Karamanai: Chellammal's birth village, suburb of Thiruvananthapuram in Kerala state.

Vadiveeswaram: village of in-laws, suburb of Nagercoil, 67.5 km from Thiruvananthapuram, and now in the state of Tamil Nadu. The two main streets mentioned in the journal are Dalawa Street and Palla Street.

Ramavarmapuram: upscale suburb of Nagercoil where Chellammal stayed with Chidambaram for a while as a newlywed when he was recuperating from Tuberculosis.

***

A Few Words About Me

I, Chellammal, am an ordinary Indian citizen. But I think no rule says that only famous people get to write their life stories. I doubt whether the newcomers in our street are even aware of my existence. I am not in the habit of initiating a conversation and making an effort to get to know people. Over the past few years, I have started to become even more withdrawn as I have developed an inferiority complex and get the feeling that due to my age younger people may not respect me.

As a policy, I believe in speaking the truth. In my opinion, in my life story also I should write only unadulterated truth. So I have decided not to write about some confidential and unsavoury matters in this journal. I am writing this for my family, especially for my children—perhaps my difficult life may seem to them like an interesting tale. I am not the kind of person who can write in one go. My body also does not permit me these days to sit and write continuously. Moreover, there are days when I just don't get the time to write. Hence, I am not sure if I will be able to complete it. As I am getting old I may even die before I finish writing this. I wish my children could read this when I am still alive. Not sure if my wish will get fulfilled. I hope the readers will excuse any errors in my language. After all, I did not have formal training or attend classes in school to learn Tamil. Only after I moved to Vadiveeswaram[1] did I teach myself the Tamil alphabet and learned to read and write in Tamil.

I have now completely forgotten to read and write Malayalam—the language of my childhood days. My proficiency in Malayalam has diminished so much that I cannot even read a Malayalam magazine with ease, surprising, considering that Malayalam was the language of instruction in my school until I reached the eighth grade; at which point I stopped going to school altogether. I had to stop school because I was expected to attain menarche soon. In my times a girl had to be married before she attained puberty. This made the family search desperately for a prospective groom to get the girl out of the house before the Brahmin village (Karamanai) started the inevitable finger-pointing. I was married when I was 13. People around the town had already begun the malicious gossip saying, "This girl looks like she has come of age. How come they have not got her married as yet? Don't they have any sense of shame or honour?" The custom in those days was to get the girls married between the ages of 10 and 13. I believe my mother got married when she was seven. Although I was only 13 I looked older. However, I started my first period only six months after I got married.

I was considered to be a beauty (by both women and men alike) in my village. People from my hometown who

---

[1] Translator's note: she was probably 14 then

saw me many years later used to comment, "What happened to you? Can't recognize you. You used to look so radiant." Or remark, "How come you have lost all that beauty?" Even I wondered how my appearance had changed. Now, of course, that I am older, I feel I look ugly with a hollow face, thin arms and excess fat around my waist. By the time I was 62, I had an entire set of false teeth. The set was loose and would come off when I laughed hard! These are the tricks time plays on you, I suppose. However, for some reason, my hair never turned grey. Only recently a few strands of grey have appeared in my hair. Come the month of *Aadi* (22 June to 22 July) I will be 74. My birth star is Rohini.[2]

****

---

[2] Rohini is Aldebaran, a binary star, one component of which is a red giant, the brightest star in the constellation Taurus.

Memories of My Parental Home and Matchmaking for My Marriage

For the matchmaking, there was only one horoscope that they considered and this was received through my father's Mami, his maternal aunt, whose parental home was in Vadiveeswaram. Manni (that is what we called my mother instead of Amma although it was the way one addressed one's elder brother's wife) used to lament to Ponna Mami (that is the way all of us addressed Mami), "My Appa has passed away before my daughter's marriage. I would not have had any worries had my father been alive. This girl is so unlucky."

"Don't you worry," Ponna Mami would reassure her, "your daughter is so beautiful that a portrait can be painted of her. There is a boy I know, where I live. But he is rather dark. He has passed BA Honours with a first-class. The boy's father, Chattai, is a lawyer with a good income. The family has considerable property. They own a house, land and much more. His first wife had two sons and two daughters and Subbu, that is her name, died a few days after she delivered the fourth child. The second wife is very soft-natured. Chattai, in general, follows the instructions from his older daughter, while her husband, the son-in-law, handles most of the family affairs. Chattai has three sons by his second wife and they are quite young. Chattai being a lawyer, the clients bring in plenty of good payments in kind, mangoes, jackfruits, plantains and the like. Your daughter will have plenty to eat, but there is only one thing that bothers me, the two girls in the family have a reputation of being 'difficult' and poor Chellammal may find it hard to deal with them."

My mother interjected, "Anyway, we haven't even looked at the horoscopes. The rest will come later."

Ponna Mami said, "They have already got her horoscope through someone. When my son-in-law had gone to Vadiveeswaram a few days ago, he had visited Chattai's house." (Ponna Mami's elder sister and brother lived just a few houses away from that of this gentleman Chattai) 'I believe Parur Subbaiyer's granddaughter is related to your mother-in-law. Contractor Appuvaiyer gave her horoscope to us. It matches very well with our son's horoscope. Do you know anything about the girl? And what kind of people are they?' They asked him." Ponna Mami added that her son-in-law Shankaran had told them, "They are very nice people. The girl is classy and you won't be able to say no to her when you see her. But the family won't be able to fulfil your expectations concerning dowry."

Mami lived in the next street with her daughter's family. She visited us often. She gave the boy's horoscope to my father saying her son-in-law had brought it. I believe it was shown to the astrologer and he had said that the horoscopes matched very well. So my father went to

Vadiveeswaram to meet the boy's family. When he returned he told my mother, "The older daughter did all the talking. Chattai hardly spoke. She has demanded as dowry 3,000 rupees plus silver vessels and a gold waist string for the boy at the time of the Diwali festival. By the way, it is true the boy is quite dark."

I want to say something at this juncture. My sisters-in-law always thought of me as stupid and ill-informed. On the contrary, I believe that I am extremely intelligent! If that were not the case I would not have remembered the details and significance of events that happened when I was so young. At the same time I was very naïve—may be that is why they perceived me as stupid. I will talk about the humiliations I suffered at my in-laws' later. Coming back to my wedding negotiations, my father left the prospective bridegroom's house saying that he would discuss the proposal with his family and get back to them. My mother said, "My father is also not there. Otherwise, he would have supported us in every way possible. How can we meet their demands? It would be very difficult. Perhaps the best option is to find a schoolteacher or marry her off as a second wife to someone."

Those days the schoolteachers my mother referred to hardly made 25 rupees a month. Within four days of my father's visit to Vadiveeswaram, the elder sister of the groom and her husband visited us. They arrived rather unexpectedly. I was wearing an old faded skirt with a *melakku*, the traditional half-sari, and had tied my hair with a thread. I had long hair. My mother was stunned and speechless on seeing visitors arrive unannounced. They introduced themselves.

She, my prospective sister-in-law, said, "We have come from Vadiveeswaram. Kesava Iyer (referring to my father, who was not at home then) visited us a few days ago. He must have told you about our conversation." By now my mother knew who they were and had started going through the motions of the traditional welcome of the prospective groom's family that was expected of her. She could give them only some fruits and coffee as they had come unexpectedly. Soon after Manni and Seethai (my prospective sister-in-law) started haggling about the details of the dowry. Sister-in-law laid out the demands—3,000 rupees as dowry, two tumblers with two deep saucers (meant for drinking coffee), a deep bowl popularly known as "Mysore chatty", a "kooja" water carrier, a lamp, a platter, a plate, vessels needed to perform ablutions, all in silver and so on. I don't exactly remember what else she asked for. She went on to detail the gold jewellery they expected to be given to the girl, "Four bangles, a two-string chain, the *thirumangalyam* chain for the groom to tie around the bride's neck during the marriage, and, six months after the marriage, a waist chain for the boy…"

Manni held her ground and repeatedly said, "We are a large family. We cannot afford to give so much. We can only come up with 2,000 rupees, a few gold bangles, a chain, some silver vessels, excluding lamp and tumbler. We have many bronze vessels that we can give…"

Seethai said, "We are not asking for too much because we know your circumstances. We came here because we heard your daughter is good looking…and indeed, it is only for that reason we are decreasing our demands. There are many families back home that are willing to strike an alliance with our family and are willing to give hundred sovereigns of gold jewellery, 5,000 rupees plus lots of silver, bronze and brass vessels to boot. As a matter of fact, if we settle for too little then our neighbours will start gossiping and speculate as to why we accepted so little as dowry. (I have to say here that what she said was true—it is very common for villagers to make such comments.) My father is a much-respected person in the village."

But nothing my prospective sister-in-law said could rattle Manni. She said, "Your family is wealthy. We are not in a position to meet your expectations." They kept arguing back and forth and finally the visitors left.

When Appa, my father, returned from work, Manni told him what had happened. He said, "Maybe they are so taken by our girl's beauty that they may come back. Let that be. But one good thing is that even though the boy is quite dark he has sharp features, so let us hope our girl will like him."

Manni continued, "What does this little girl know? Indeed, our girl should consider herself lucky if they come back. Considering our circumstances, we cannot have great expectations for an alliance with such a good family where she will have plenty to eat, can wear nice clothes, and who knows, keeping in mind the honour of the family, they may also buy her jewellery so that she has the same status as the other women." Hearing Manni created a sense of great expectation and awe in me.

Appa then posed a question, "It will be a large joint family, will our girl be able to cope?"

Manni replied, "She probably would not have to stay with the family too long. The boy is educated, he will find a good job and move out. And certainly, he will take her along with him."

Appa interjected, "Anyway we will see if they return, but do not agree to their unreasonable demands. That will create hardship for us." So saying he left to deal with other tasks he had on hand.

Just as Appa had predicted, the groom's family came back the next day. The sister was the spokesperson again. She said that we should somehow come up with the silver tumbler and the gold waist chain for the boy, but that they would settle for a gold chain of lesser value. That day they had another person, a mutual friend of our family, with them. He addressed my mother in familiar terms and tried to persuade her, "Manni Ammalu, you should consider yourselves fortunate for forming this alliance. Don't let the opportunity slip. The girl has crossed the marriageable age. How long will you keep the girl at home? Consider what I am saying. The groom is well educated and comes from a good family. There are others who have much less and who would ask for much more. Considering their status, they are not asking for much. I have known them for many years. Settle this and move on."

I don't remember that relative's name. Appa was at home that day. With Appa's approval, Manni agreed to give 2,250 rupees instead of 3,000 rupees. As for the silver tumblers, she agreed to provide them in instalments during functions and ceremonies that would usually be conducted after the wedding. My prospective in-laws accepted the deal and said, "Tomorrow is an auspicious day for the engagement. 'Residency' Ramaiyer is my father's elder cousin. We will bring him along. Please prepare milk sweet and coconut milk sweet for the occasion. We will be here in the evening." (I think they said they would come at 4 p.m.)

Then my mother asked, "Wouldn't the boy and his father want to see the girl?"

The sister quickly replied, "My father will accept my choice and that goes for my brother too!"

Ramaiyer, whom Seethai had mentioned, lived in the Puthan Market area. The next evening Seethai and her husband Natarajan, Ramaiyer and a few others arrived for the engagement ceremony. My mother had prepared the milk sweet and the coconut milk sweet, and kept the sweets in the Mysore silver bowl and a bronze bowl for the occasion. My elder sister Meena did my hair and tied a decorative golden ornament at the end of my long plait. I wore the only silk skirt and *melaakku* I had. In those days we did not care about matching colours.

Seethai had brought along two ladies one of whom was Ramaiyer's wife. The other one was his daughter-in-law, Kamakshi. She was the maternal aunt of my mother's youngest brother's wife. So we knew her from before. Kamakshi sang the praises of my future in-laws and said that I was lucky to be marrying into such a family. She told us that they were a close-knit family, and that they were wealthy. My father-in-law had recently purchased land, owned five houses and earned at least 500 rupees per month.

Manni whispered, "We really don't know so much about the family. People tend to exaggerate. In any case, this boy will only inherit one fifth." Kamakshi went to the corridor to be with her people. Manni saw me standing there. She turned towards me and said, "Go inside. You don't need to listen to our conversations. This is not meant for children. Apply some powder on your face, and wear the gold chain and ornaments."

I told her, "I can wear them only if you give them to me." She got up and took out the Rangoon diamond ear studs (I normally wore simple gold studs), the heavy two-string gold chain and four gold bangles.

Here I have to explain something. Manni, over the years, had been buying jewellery including a necklace, waistband and armbands, a hairpiece and such, all in gold. She loved jewellery and at that time gold cost only 13 rupees per sovereign. Manni would never like wasting money on clothes and would say that only gold had lasting value. So, whenever she bought clothing it was made of durable tough material, and the amount was enough for only one or two dresses at a time. I will write later about my mother and my family. She even joined "chit funds" (community savings funds) to buy jewellery. This way, she had collected quite a few pieces. She always said that the jewellery belonged to everyone and that the girls could take turns to wear them for occasions but that they did not belong to any one person. It seemed like she did not want any of us to lay claims on them and maybe that was the reason she did not let me wear more jewellery from the common pool on the engagement day. Or maybe she wanted me to look simple that day.

Now let me try to explain my feelings about people coming to "see" me before the marriage. I did not have any specific thoughts about marriage. However, there was some kind of fear. Marriages were arranged by parents in those days according to their wishes. One had to quietly accept whoever they chose. But the marriage had to be done before the girl came of age. I knew I was getting older, getting past the marriageable age after which it was not considered appropriate to continue living with one's parents. I did not think I had a choice. My main fear was about leaving my home and going to live with strangers. Another fear was about sex. I had heard bits and pieces about sex from some of my friends in the village. I was thirteen, so I could think and understand. Some of my friends were younger when they got married and I wonder if they even grasped any of the implications.

As I was getting lost in my thoughts, Manni brought me back to the moment, "Don't just stand there. Go and do *namaskarams* to the elders but don't linger on." What Manni wanted to really convey was this: Seethai may enquire about my education and singing.

In those days it was adequate if a girl knew to read and write. Rarely did girls complete their high school education. So Seethai was likely to ask me if I knew how to sing and also ask up to which class I had studied. She may even ask if I knew how to cook. Manni was worried that Seethai would come up with a barrage of questions and I may give some silly replies and that is why she did not want me there with the groom's party for too long.

I really cannot remember what questions Seethai asked me that day. We had not invited any outsiders to the engagement ceremony. I do remember that Manni skillfully avoided firm commitments to Seethai's demands.

After the guests left, my mother, father and sister discussed the itemized expenses for the wedding.

My sister Meena stayed nearby in Srikandeswaram with her husband and her only daughter. Her married life was short-lived. My brother-in-law died within two years of my wedding. My sister was seven years older than me; she was the oldest of the siblings. She had a very tough life. After her husband passed away she came back to her parental home. In those days once a woman became a widow, all she was considered good for was the household chores. Widows could not go out freely and had to stay indoors for many years.

Meena was averse to sex. Soon after her nuptials, she had to stay with us for nearly two years. (I am not sure if it was exactly two years but it was probably.) At that time, I think my brother-in-law was working or studying in Hyderabad. He used to come by occasionally to visit her. As soon as he arrived she would go hide and try to avoid him. He would bring her cosmetics like face powder, lotion, ribbons, etc. He was tall and fair and a very handsome man. He also used to look very smart in modern clothes. My sister was also very good-looking and had a good figure. I was the plump one in my family with excess fat around my waist (it was not too obvious when I was young). During my brother-in-law's visits, it was a tremendous problem for my mother to persuade my sister to sleep with her husband. It was also difficult to convince her to go with her husband and visit his family home. She would start crying and my mother had to plead with her.

My brother-in-law Veeraraghavan's place was in Vanjiyur, not too far from our place. He was the youngest of four brothers and their father had died when my brother-in-law was still young. Their native place was Palakkaadu in Kerala but they had shifted to Thiruvananthapuram when my brother-in-law was still a child. He had grown up and received education in Thiruvananthapuram. They had some property. All the brothers were educated and were graduates. My brother-in-law had done his BSc and for a short time, he worked as a teacher in a local school in Thiruvananthapuram.

I remember my sister and her husband living across from our house for a while. That was when they had a baby girl. He had become very thin and frail then. He was very fond of the baby and took good care of her. Even if the child was a little sick, he would not leave her and be next to her, frequently checking if she had a temperature. My sister and he had frequent arguments. I do not know the reasons but I knew he was a good man. My sister seemed to not care about him. Even when he was sick, she was not there to help him. Instead, being very much into religion, she was more interested in visiting her favourite temples. She was also blindly religious and orthodox. Finally, when he passed away she was not next to him. Instead, she was at our house.

I heard that my brother-in-law had some problems with his heart. His legs became swollen, he was incapacitated and later he died. His family performed many religious rituals to pray for his cure. Only later did I realize the foolishness of such rituals. In those days medicine was not advanced like it is now. When my brother-in-law died, he was 30 years old and my sister Meena was barely 22; the baby was about three years old.

Just like Meena wished, it turned out that she had to live permanently in the house where she was born and raised. She cried some on hearing the news of his passing but I don't think it affected her much. I was deeply saddened by his death. He was very loving and kind to me. He endearingly called me *angichi*, "little sister", or addressed me as they would address a child. I used to take his gifts, like the powder and lotion, that my sister would throw away. My parents would never buy these things for us and rarely did we get some face powder. I had to make one box last for up to a whole year, so I was thrilled to get these throwaways from my sister. I was about seven or eight years old then. Once my brother-in-law saw my worn-out skirt and promised he would bring cotton material for two skirts the next time he came and he did bring for me enough material to stitch two more. His life got over six months after my nuptials. It was the end of an epoch.

As time passed Meena realized her mistakes and started feeling his loss and was deeply saddened. Meena had learnt music and could sing fairly well. She was extremely good with all the housework, including cooking. She would cook and clean with great relish, and would not let anyone help her. Even if we had a whole slew of visitors she would get to work and manage everything all by herself. She could use the stone grinder with ease. Even after she became old this was one thing that she never hesitated to do.

I remember one detail now. In 1993 she visited me. I used to pay to get the ground batter for *dosai*. She refused to let me do that. She would say, "This is such a small quantity, why do you need to have it done by someone else? This is no problem at all. I will do it for you," and immediately get to work and grind the rice flour into a fine batter. The batter would be so good that the *idli*s, that were made the next day, would be soft, like flower petals. She was 77 then and I was stunned to see that she could still use the stone grinder with such ease.

I do not know Meena's exact date of birth. All I knew was she was seven years older than me and I do not even clearly know the year I was born. I know I was born under the star Rohini in the month of Aadi. I knew my age only because Manni told me my age. I haven't seen my horoscope. I searched for it but could not find it in the house. In those days they used the local lunar calendar year for the year of birth. This must have been so since we belonged to Thiruvananthapuram, Kerala, where this was the practice. Even Kanyakumari was then with Kerala. So, they set the horoscopes the same way here also. Meena was usually very honest except when she was asked about her age. She would always decrease it by two or three years when answering. Most women tend to lie about their age. I know of some who will decrease their age by almost ten years with no qualms!

Meena was usually up by 4 a.m. She would go to the river for her daily bath and would return and briskly start the day's chores. She enjoyed working and never complained. I have never seen her lazy or tired. On the rare occasion when she came down with a fever or a headache, she would still go ahead with her daily routine of an early morning bath followed by work. She showed enormous affection towards her parents and siblings. She never seemed to dwell on the misfortunes in her personal life. Over time she and Manni started having arguments. The main cause for these arguments was Manni. Meena liked coffee and used to have four cups a day. Manni would object and complain about the cost. She also was upset that Meena used up supplies too quickly and would say she was consuming too much milk, using too much coconut in her cooking and so on. Since Meena was very orthodox she would keep pouring water everywhere to purify the place for something or the other and Manni would pick on that too. Meena would then get upset and protest by going on a fast for two to three days. Then Manni would have to pacify her, apologize and persuade her to eat again. Peace would then prevail for a few days and then they would go at it again.

Meena had no financial help from her in-laws after her husband's death. They did help her some for her daughter's wedding. I don't know how much though. My brother-in-law's three brothers lived up to 80 years of age. The eldest one lived up to 90, in fact. Meena's mother-in-law died after she was 85. It is a pity my brother-in-law died at such a young age.

Meena would draw beautiful *kolam*s, the threshold designs done every morning, using dry rice powder and rice flour paste. Although she did not keep flowers in her hair (unfortunately, she could not wear flowers as a widow) she would tie flowers and decorate everybody's hair, especially mine. She would decorate my hair and darn the fragrant *thazhampoo* and screw pine on my plait. She used to make different ornaments with flowers, but it never seemed to bother her, even at that young age, that she couldn't wear them. She would weave beautiful things with shiny beads—dolls, baskets, little chairs, etc. I felt that she was attached to my mother but the affection was not reciprocated adequately. In general, Manni was not very attached to her daughters except maybe to her youngest. Even that I am not too sure about.

****

Karamanai: My Early Life with My Parents and Grandparents

My youngest sister, Krishna, was born a year after I got married. My parents had eight children, four girls and four boys. Strangely enough, I have never seen my parents being close or having intimate conversations. Obviously, love and affection are not necessary to create babies. Even animals reproduce.

There was no system of contraception in those days. However poor the people were, there was no dearth of children. By the time one child was weaned off breast milk, the wife was already pregnant with the next baby. The women of those days were used to this. My parents did not have their separate place to sleep. My mother slept in a corner of the passage between the entrance and the living quarters and we children slept on the floor, leaving a little space for getting around, in the middle room. I think my father slept in the vestibule area, next to the outer door of the house. At times father would come to sleep with my mother and I would hear some noises (more like sighs) from my mother. I was curious and wanted to get up and see what was going on, but was afraid. In those days the wives tried to please their husbands irrespective of whether they liked sex or not. That is what I have heard most women say. Just like hunger, this lust was a desire and need that had to be fulfilled. When my father came to her, mother would say, "The little girl (referring to me) is getting of age, it will be shameful if she finds us in this situation." It did not seem like my father paid any heed to that plea.

Our bed consisted of a single mat, one pillow and a blanket on the floor. There were plenty of bed bugs on the wall. Father would go around with an oil lamp, pick one bug at a time and put it in the flame. To start with, we did not have electricity. Instead, we had kerosene lamps. We got the first electric lamp in our house ten years after electricity came to our town. We were also late in getting water taps. The first water tap that was laid was laid outside our house in the street. You just had to touch it for the water to spurt out as if from an elephant's trunk. I could now effortlessly fill multiple pots and buckets with water and store them in the house. I was ecstatic that I did not have to carry a pot on my hip to the river to fetch water anymore. Previously I had to go at least twice a day to the river to fetch water. I had to climb down the steps (and when the river was running low I had to go down more steps). Most people in the village would carry the water pots when they went to the river for their daily baths. Our street was the closest to the river, so maybe my chore was a little easier. I remember at least once or twice the river water flowed into our street and right up to our doorstep after heavy rains.

I am elaborating on all this because to me it seemed that all the difficulties of day-to-day living did not seem to bother my parents when it came to making babies. The bed bugs and the hard bed did not seem to matter. The women accepted the situation saying that god "gave" them the children. As mentioned above, my mother had eight children in quick succession. After my wedding, at the age of 40, she had my youngest sister Krishna, and right after that, she went into menopause. If not, she might have had two more.

My mother wasn't overweight, wasn't too tall. With a fair complexion, she was just the right size and walked with a straight back. She used to apply natural products like flour made from a variety of grains, turmeric and such on her face. Only much later in her life did she start using soap. Her face was smooth and unblemished. Even her arms and legs were smooth and glowing. Her diamond studs and nose ornament went very well with her beautiful complexion. She wore a large round *kunkumam pottu*[3] on her forehead. Everyone in the street said that her appearance was goddess Mahalaxmi incarnate. She usually wore a cheap five-rupee sari. She had only two or three of them. She also had two or three silk saris that she only wore on special occasions.

In those days we did not have too many clothes for daily wear, but usually, we had a few silk saris stored away. We did not have the variety that you see today. Manni was very smart, very frugal, and quite enterprising. She

---

[3] *Kunkumam* is a powder, usually red colored, containing turmeric, that is considered very auspicious when worn as a "*pottu*" (dot) on the forehead by Hindu women.

was very good with calculations and could do them in her head without using paper. She even started lending money and charging interest. I cannot blame her—she was in a difficult situation. One item she would not skimp on was milk. She would always buy ample quantities of milk. I remember that when I was pregnant with my son (Ambi, my second child) and visited, we even had two cows in our house. My mother did not like the watered-down milk she had to buy on the street and this was her solution.

I want to share another example of my mother's frugality. If we children had four days off from school, she would take us to our grandparents' house, which was three kilometres away. Sometimes the four days off would be extended to eight days. She did not mind if I missed school but she made sure the boys always attended school. My school was in Karamanai. Our grandparents lived in Pazhavangadi. Once, my brothers, Sundar and Subramaniam started going to Vanjiyoor School, close to where my grandparents lived, it made things easy for Mami. She could just let them stay and go to school from their grandparents' place. There was no rush to bring them home to Karamanai. As long as we stayed at my grandparents' place she could save on food and coffee. Usually, for our journey home, grandpa would send us in a horse carriage with plenty of food—rice, lentils, coconut, vegetables and such. He would also pay the one and a half rupee cost for the ride. I don't remember seeing such a carriage anywhere else. There was a place for four adults to sit facing one another. If there were small kids, two or three more could be taken in the carriage. But then there would be no place to keep the baggage. I enjoyed those horse carriage rides. The funny part is that when Manni took us from Karamanai to visit our grandparents, she would make us walk. Manni's sisters-in-law (by marriage to her brothers) apparently used to say that if Manni visited she would return home with a month's supply of provisions. Since Manni was their husbands' sister (a position of power in the family), they would probably say that even if she took something insignificant.

Here I should tell you something about Thatha, my grandfather. Thatha was from the town of Paappakudi. Paatti, my grandmother, was from Sundarapandipuram. My grandfather was a disciple of one Coimbatore Swami. When Thatha had somehow lost his inheritance and was in a difficult financial position, Paatti's sister and her husband, who were disciples of Coimbatore Swami, introduced Thatha to him. Paatti's sister's husband was an auditor and they were quite well to do. Coimbatore Swami in turn was the disciple of the famous Ramalinga Swami and had learned a lot under his guidance. What exactly he learned or was preached to him is not clear. Coimbatore Swami had many faithful followers. Thatha would go to receive the blessings of Coimbatore Swami but he usually sat in a corner in the sea of humanity. Apparently, at some point, Paatti's sister's husband, who was rather close to the Swami, drew his attention to Thatha's financial hardships. Despite a large number of influential people waiting to receive blessings and personal advice from the Swami before he left this material world, he called in Thatha first and gave him a private audience, provided him with sage advice, reassured him that all would be well and instructed him to go to Thiruvananthapuram. Manni recounted all this to me. Thatha then arrived in Thiruvananthapuram with his family and led a glorious life for many years. He did face some financial hardship again towards the end of his life. When Manni got married at the age of seven, Thatha's disciples made sure it was a grand event.

Thatha was tall, fair, slim, and sharp-featured. Even my father-in-law used to say, "That Karur Subbaiyer has an imposing personality." Many in the neighbourhood were convinced that Thatha could cure illnesses. I am not sure what medicines he dispensed. He would pray and dispense special "butter" to be applied on wounds and also give holy *prasadam*, offerings ritualistically blessed by the deities. People believed that even if he just looked at them and blessed them it would cure them of their disease. His disciples included rich and influential people—some from the royal family like the Raja of Kollankodu and the Raja of Kochi, others like judges, Munsifs and even upper-class women known as Thamburattis. I have heard that the large house he lived in was built by some of his followers. The house had a compound. Across from the house his disciples had built another building with a central prayer hall and rooms on the sides. Thatha had six children, four boys and two girls.

Two important functions were conducted annually at my grandfather's place. One was Thiruvathirai in the month of Margazhi (December), the other was a celebration in honour of his guru in the month of Thai (January). All the disciples would congregate in his house one day before Thiruvathirai. There were also people from Nagercoil who came for the occasion. The main deity was Shiva. I think they mostly used pictures of Nataraja, the Dancing

Lord Shiva. The disciples would bring in lots of flowers, fruits, vegetables, rice and lentils as offerings. All the pictures of the gods were decorated with beautiful flowers. It was very artistic. Lord Nataraja had the most floral decorations. The fragrance of flowers and incense filled the air. That fragrance was indeed special, and I do not remember such a unique perfume even in the temples. It is possible that the sweat of people diminished the fragrance of flowers in the popular temples. Men and women stood in separate sections. One person played the harmonium, another played the drum. Everyone sang from the *Arutpa*, the songs written by Ramalinga Adigal generally referred to as Vallalar. The music itself was somewhat mediocre, but Thatha's presence was electric. He was attired in yellow silk, held a small pot of water in his right hand, and wore an anklet with bells around his left foot and raised his left foot (just like Shiva) and danced with grace. If you could see his face on those occasions, it would seem like he was in ecstasy, far removed from the present world. He would balance and dance on one leg for quite a while but I cannot remember how many hours it lasted. Later he would sit in a reclining chair reciting poems from *Arutpa*, and would explain the meaning of the poems in simple language. After the event, the disciples would come up to him one by one to pay their respects with *namaskarams*, the traditional South Indian gesture of showing respect by falling flat at the feet of gurus or elders. He would give each of them the sacred ash, but did not hand out any food. Here I should emphasize that he never discriminated between people based on their caste or social status. Among his disciples were also Ezhavars, considered an inferior caste in Kerala. Meals were served at all times of the day and night during these events. Late in the evening, there would be prayer after which the *prasadam* would be dispensed; there was no dancing at that time. Guru *pujai*, salutation to the teacher, was also done similarly. I don't remember if Thatha danced then. A huge pot would be kept outside the house and sweet rice would be prepared.

At home, Thatha had at least four or five visitors daily. They would recite the poems from *Arutpa*. Only milk and fruits were offered to the deities. He would then sing and perform *deeparadhanai*, the ritual lighting of special lamps to seek blessings, in front of the pictures of the deities and end by blessing the devotees, giving them the sacred ash. I remember the nasty comment made by my sister-in-law about this ceremony. She would say that Parur Subbaiyer (my grandfather) pinched the hands of female devotees when he gave them the *prasadam*. In those days I was so afraid of her that I could not bring myself to take a stand against this unsubstantiated innuendo about my grandfather, unsubstantiated because he usually had his eyes closed as he handed out the *prasadam* and he could not have possibly discerned who the devotee was—man, woman or child! Some of the women in Vadiveeswaram were evil and had no compunction in making baseless accusations just for the fun of it, indeed they thrived on such gossip. My sister-in-law disliked me and my family, she put them down whenever she had a opportunity. To her, that was probably like eating her favourite sweet.

Thatha died when he was 72. He had a coconut grove in Thiruvananthapuram. He spent many afternoons there cutting down the dried branches. A few days before his death, when he was doing the usual pruning, the axe fell on his leg causing a deep wound. After that injury, he couldn't walk very well. I do not know what kind of treatment he got for the injury. In those days I did not think deeply about possible causes, but much later I wondered whether the wound got infected. I remember having mentioned this to Manni. She replied, "That is possible." I asked her how come he could cure many people but was unable to cure his own ailment. She replied that he was a pious man, "god-like," and he might have decided that he did not want to continue this worldly life. She said that I should not be asking such questions about a saintly individual like him.

Manni, was not like the average women of those days of the *agraharam*, the Brahmin section of the neighbourhood. She did not frequent the temples like the others, she was not into religious fasts, and she did not believe in mythological stories. Even Ramalinga Swami has said that mythologies are not really true happenings. She did believe in the alignments of stars and auspicious days but did not care about astrology. She was not orthodox either. She also had some belief in rituals, and we did have pictures of the gods in our house. Most important was the picture of the dancing god Shiva Nataraja. Milk was the offering of choice to the god. Every day between 7 and 8 p.m., we would gather and sing a few songs from *Arutpa*, that we had learnt. Then Manni would light camphor cubes, make the offering to the god and then each of us would make the customary gestures of placing our hands over the camphor flame and then to our eyes to accept the blessings. Manni would also hand out the sacred ash. On festival days there would be an extra session of the same ritual in the afternoon when we would also have treats like *payasam*, sweet milk and rice pudding and savoury *vadai*, deep fried lentil donuts.

When Thatha died, people from the village showed up to offer condolences to Paatti. Some said, "Ramasubbi, how sad that you have to face such an awful situation. Despite your having reached a ripe old age (she was 67 then), he beat you in leaving for the next world. Surely a virtuous woman like you should have been blessed by being allowed to leave this world before him, while still being able to wear the flowers and *pottu*, the prerogative of a married woman. Probably this is due to bad karma from a previous life."

Paatti used to reply tersely, "Yes, I am not that fortunate." After they would leave she would say, "These people are idiots, I didn't come into this world tethered to him; our bond happened later. Anyway, he was not all that affectionate or caring towards me. He used to scold me for mistakes made by others. Even the most affectionate couple do not die together. His time was up and he has gone. These people are making these comments as though they are going to provide for me!"

Paatti was a beautiful woman. She had a wonderful, fair, smooth complexion, and a graceful figure. She never got angry. She would say that we should not hurt anyone, even our enemies. I have never seen her being rude to anyone. Every morning she would recite some prayers (she knew many Sanskrit prayers) while rolling the quartz crystal prayer beads. She was into visiting temples but usually did not observe any religious fasts. She did not seem too sad about my grandfather's passing. Despite that, she followed the local custom and tonsured her head, as was required for a Brahmin widow. She said, "I have tonsured my head because of these stupid people." In those days—even very young widows—among many other things they lost because of widowhood, widows also lost their hair and remained tonsured for the rest of their life. When I was young, I did not give it much thought. Only later in life did I realize what a terrible injustice this was towards women. I also felt extremely sad whenever I encountered these widows.

As I started thinking about these issues, I questioned Paatti (she died at the age of 87, I was 30 then) and asked her why she followed these customs when she had told us many times that tonsuring the head for the sake of a husband, religious fasts and other rituals were irrational. She replied, "I have no faith in those customs, but have submitted to the pressures of society. These people would torture me saying, 'Ramasubbi is so old and knows the *shastras* very well. Even then she has not shaved her hair. Isn't this a sin?' Same goes for these fasts. Shastras have prescribed so many kinds of fasts for women. Even if you don't keep other fasts you have to keep the Rishi Panchami fast after menopause. It is a fast for those born as women—especially Brahmin women—for the end of menstruation so that we don't suffer similarly in the next birth."

I used to get very upset listening to all this but usually avoided getting into an argument with Paatti. In general, I felt she wasn't bitter about being subjected to these customs and she seemed to take it in her stride, so I decided to not push it any further. But I just could not get it off my mind. We are born with our hair and it seemed so unjust for someone to force one to remove it. If the wife dies the man goes on to remarry and have a merry life and they do this even when they are quite old. Men are so selfish and self-centred. They wrote all these rules and customs to be followed by society, and I have no doubt they wrote them to their advantage. A female child is considered to have achieved womanhood when she starts her periods. In those days they used to celebrate this occasion with great fanfare. Even now other castes lavishly celebrate this. This is what makes a woman a woman; it is her identity. To consider this a sin seemed to me the height of stupidity. Do they want to be born as men in the next birth or as Aravanis? I have read about the plight of Aravanis. They are not even seen as human beings and they suffer unspeakable humiliation and are treated as untouchables. To think that something god-given or nature-given which is the very identity of women was being degraded like this by a community annoyed me immensely. Will all the post-menopausal women who observe the Rishi Panchami ritual fast be born as Aravanis or men? Or maybe they will not be reborn. Whatever it is, if their wish comes true, it will put an end to the Brahmin community. No man can be born without a woman. Even though Paatti appeared rational, even she seemed afraid to take a stand and oppose the social norms.

Soon after Thatha's passing Paatti had cataract operations in both her eyes. For almost two years she had managed with very poor vision and was almost blind. My mother had told me a story about how Thatha's reputation about curing diseases began with his curing someone who had a wooden sliver lodged in the eye. Why didn't Thatha, who cured so many people of their diseases, bother to help Paatti get her vision back? These thoughts occurred to me much later in life. Paatti had brought in 5,000 rupees as *stridhan*, wealth or gifts received by a woman from her parental home. In those days that was a substantial amount. Whether she had later saved that money in a bank or loaned it to earn interest, I do not know. She told me that she used that money for her eye operation. Her vision became very clear after the operation and stayed clear till she died. Even her doctor Joseph was surprised at how well she did.

Paatti was a very calm and composed person. When my father passed away, Paatti was in our house in Karamanai. Chithi (my husband's stepmother) had come to offer condolences. She saw Paatti and kept commenting on how good looking she was even at her age. Paatti used to have an oil bath—she applied oil on her body from head to toe—twice a week. Once (after Thatha's demise) I went to visit Paatti at her place in Pazhavangadi. Thatha's four sons had divided the place among themselves and lived there. The main house had a compound. Three of the sons shared this and the houses were in a row with partitions in between. Across from this was the house that the oldest son now occupied, which included the prayer hall where Thatha originally prayed and held all the religious functions. That was also the place where Thatha used to meet his devotees and danced. Paatti spent three months out of a year with each son.

I stepped into the eldest son's house looking for her. I had barely asked my aunt where Paatti was when my aunt snapped at me and curtly said, "Your Paatti is near the well having her oil bath. She has oiled herself from head to toe. She will use only Pears soap. Why does she need all this at her age?" She continued, "You used to look so radiant and beautiful. (I was 27 or 28 years old then.) How come all that is gone? I have heard that your sisters-in-law are difficult people. Even the men in Vadiveeswaram I heard are pretty tough to deal with. How are you coping? Take care."

I merely answered, "I do not know what you are saying," and left it at that. People in my family did gossip about the behaviour of certain women of Vadiveeswaram and I had also heard families on my street talk about it. They used to talk about an affair between my father-in-law and a Brahmin lady—I truly do not know whether that really happened.

In general, as far as sex is concerned, they made much of it when a woman had affairs. Even today they emphasize the need for a woman to guard her chastity. This also is reinforced and perhaps even exaggerated in the movies. Even when a woman loses her chastity due to rape she is considered a lowly human being. By the same token, a married man can be a respected citizen even when he openly engages in an affair and sets up a separate house, referred to in Tamil as *chinna veedu* or "small house" for his beloved. A young widow, who could be just 16 years old, is still shown in the movies wearing a plain white sari with no jewellery. The same applies to the traditional wedding pendant (*thali*) sentiment. This *thali* sentiment seems to be more often depicted in Tamil movies than in other languages. In North India, apart from Maharashtra, they do not consider the bestowal of the *thali* (called *mangalsutra* in the North) on the bride as an important part of the ritual. The most important and universal (Hindu) wedding ritual is the one where the couple takes seven steps in front of the sacred fire. That is the key part of marriage, sanctified by law and tradition. So I wonder why these Tamil films give so much importance to the *thali*. Have men in olden times managed to create this feeling in women that the husband's very life resides in the *thali* which then got reflected in films? People could argue that the *thali* was a visible sign to indicate that a woman was married and some sort of protection for her. If so, then why is it that the men do not have to wear a similar symbol showing that they are married? Nowadays, the wealthier women make a nice designer gold chain and attach the *thali* pendant to it. Usually, the *thali* lies hidden under the sari, and then the chain looks like a chain that anyone would wear, married or unmarried, so this argument about the *thali* being a recognizable sign is invalid. The fate of the not-so-wealthy woman is quite terrible. She will not have her gold *thali* chain for too long. The usually worthless husband would have sold the gold to buy his liquor. Many of these poor men are alcoholics.

Paatti also used to say that there was no mention of the *thali* custom in the *shastras*. Paatti was, after all, an astute woman. Of her six children, I believe my mother was the most intelligent. I have never seen my Thatha and Paatti having a conversation, and so I wonder how they had six children. All six were born before they moved to Thiruvananthapuram. Only after he arrived in Thiruvananthapuram did Thatha start exhibiting the qualities of a holy man. That is when he also started having a steady income, which progressively increased. However, towards the end, he did face some financial problems. The huge house started looking somewhat dilapidated. The change of fortune did not seem to affect Paatti that much. The number of disciples started dwindling. He did not live much longer. It was Paatti's serene face, her intellect and her fair complexion that captivated me.

Caught up in such thoughts I walked towards the backyard and sure enough, as per my aunt's description mentioned earlier, I found Paatti near the well, anointed with sesame oil from head to toe, bathing with Pears soap, leisurely drawing pot after pot of water from the well and pouring it on herself. I told her about my aunt's comments. She replied, "That is the way these people talk. I buy my own oil and soap, after all. As long as we live, we need to take care of our body and keep the skin clean from itchy rashes and scabies. I don't really bother about remarks made by people. Immature people will talk in this manner." She continued, "How come you have lost weight and your complexion has turned dark? I have always told you, haven't I, not to care about what anyone says and to eat well whenever you can. You have been married for over 12 years now. You have two children (my third child, Kumar, was born two years after Paatti passed away, and seven years later, Kanchana was born). Don't be too timid. You are very smart, you ask intelligent questions, do not let your in-laws treat you like a loser. Even if they are offensive give them the right answer without getting angry. You should let them know that you have rights in that family. That doesn't mean you have to quarrel with them." So, she went on.

I gave it back to her saying, "You and Manni had preached to me soon after my wedding, 'You should be sober and not aggressive in your marital family. Do not argue; just listen and obey. Sisters-in-law are probably not going to be pleasant. Apparently, they are a close-knit family and they don't seem to differentiate between the children of the first and second wife. You should not be a cause for discord in their unity. The son-in-law (referring to my husband) is well educated. He will soon find a job with a good salary and will move out with you. It will only be a short time before that happens, so try to cope.' With repeated advice like this, all of you made me afraid and spineless. My husband followed in his father's footsteps. He became a lawyer like his father and started practice in the same town along with his father. It is ten years now since he got his degree and started going to court. Only now he has started getting an income of 200 to 300 rupees. Ultimately, he will never move out of the house, let alone out of the town, and I am going to be stuck in the joint family."

Paatti listened to what I said and replied, "Don't be so timid. As I told you before, it has been over 12 years since you got married. The children are growing up. I heard that your in-laws are trying to prevent the children from bonding with you. Ammalu Manni gave me this information. She said that this is being done by your sisters-in-law. Your intelligence and beauty are being masked, like a lamp inside a pot. Your husband has an income. Have him get you whatever you desire. Make sure your children are close to you. Do not care about what anybody says. Try to be happy. I will pray for a good future for you. I do not know how much longer I will be around. I hope I have a quick end and not get bedridden, that is all I am hoping for now." That was the last advice Paatti gave me. Paatti passed away within two years of that conversation. I saw her only once during those two years.

Paatti came often from Pazhavangadi to Karamanai by bus on her own. Once when she came she got off at the wrong stop. "The conductor said 'stop please' and I got off. I kept walking but the Aandiyirakkam bus stop (the bus stop for Karamanai) never seemed to come. Then I checked with someone and realized I had got off at the wrong stop. And that person brought me up to Aandiyirakkam." I believe everyone laughed aloud when Paatti said "stop please." Not just then but whenever we thought of Paatti we thought of that and laughed.

Paatti was 87 when she died. She had a short bout of a diarrhea-like illness and died. I got to know about her death only two days later and went to Pazhavangadi. The sons conducted an elaborate ceremony after her death with her own money. Paatti really did not care for these ceremonies. All she wanted was a peaceful, happy life. She felt that children, even if they do not help much, should avoid causing pain to their ageing parents. She did not care about what they did for her after she was gone. While she was alive, she had to endure the loss of her daughter, a daughter-in-law, a son-in-law (my father), and the husband of one of her granddaughters. She was saddened but would comfort herself by saying, "Their time is done and they had to leave."

Now I remember something that Paatti said when my father died. It was almost four or five days since his passing. All of us were still in deep sorrow. We were lying around listless, unable to do anything. Paatti commented,

"How much longer are you people going to carry on like this, constantly crying without bathing or eating? Ammalu, listen to me. Your husband when he was around was yelling at you all the time. I have never seen him say any loving words to you. He appeared angry even as he arrived from his office in the evening. He seemed at times to be affectionate to the children but even that was not consistent. (I personally felt that my father seemed to show favouritism while dealing with children, treating one child better than the other.) All I can say is he did bring in some income. Even that is gone now. That is about it."

By the time she finished saying this Manni got very angry. She said, "How could you be so casual about the fact that he brought in some money? My whole livelihood depended on that. How am I going to care for these children? It is going to be a while before they grow up and are on their own. With all your intelligence how can you casually make a comment suggesting it was an insignificant amount?" My mother was in despair, hitting her head with her hands and crying loudly after she said all this.

Paatti retorted, "Those who are gone are not going to come back. Let us figure out a way to raise these children." I mention this incident to illustrate that nothing rattled Paatti, who was always practical and pragmatic.

Paatti never visited me in the house of my in-laws. At the time of my wedding, it was less than a year since the passing of Thatha and so she did not go out anywhere. In those days a woman was forbidden to leave the house for one year after the death of her husband. This was one of the multiple injustices perpetrated on widows. Fortunately, my mother and sister did not shave their heads when they became widows. By then the practice of widows tonsuring their heads was becoming less prevalent. My sister became a widow eight years before my father passed away. I have mentioned it elsewhere. And the only custom she did not follow was shaving off her hair. Otherwise, she gave up everything normally enjoyed by married women—wearing flowers in the hair, the *pottu*, turmeric on the face, jewellery and good clothes. Another practice that was going away at that time was the white sari that the widows were required to wear. Fortunately, my sister did not become a widow during my marriage because widows were forbidden from participating in auspicious occasions. In short, widows were expected to behave like the living dead. However, even today the state of widows has not improved sufficiently. It is still quite bad in the villages. Even now they are not allowed to actively take part in joyous functions like weddings. They still do not wear flowers, turmeric or the *pottu*. A few educated women have broken this tradition and they continue to dress the way they did before their husbands died. I hope all women will ultimately do the same, that is, continue to live and dress the same way they did before they became widows. Even in other religions—especially among Muslims—there are many restrictions for women. However, nowhere are widows considered to be as useless as among Hindus. If I start writing about the treatment of Hindu widows, I could write pages on the topic. As a matter of fact, I would like to write a separate essay on that subject, but I am not sure if I will ever find the time to do it. So, I will stop digressing and return to my autobiography.

****

My Marriage

As I have mentioned before, after my engagement, my sister Meena and Manni started working on the budget for the wedding. They made a list of things to be bought. Meena, being artistic, wanted to have a nicely decorated wedding tent and reasonably good musicians to play for the wedding. They discussed other matters; the in-laws have demanded a full set of snacks and eatables—*murukku*, *athirasam* and other sweets. Should they try to make smaller sizes—half the full size—and make it appear like the whole deal?

Meena said, "To meet their extra demands you can give away my silver and bronze vessels, they are anyway lying in storage and are of no use to me."

Manni replied, "We will do that if we absolutely need to. They seemed at that time to work so well together."

I want to mention one more interesting incident while the wedding preparations were going on. My younger sister Kunji (she was seven) and my bother Natarajan (he was four) were talking among themselves and then said to me, "Chellammal (they usually called me by my name), this is so much fun...There will be *idlis*, eatables to eat, drums will be played, all the relatives will come to our house, we will have more kids to play with. We will have so much to eat. We can't wait!" The rest of us could not help laughing listening to their gleeful chatter.

Manni was not amused. She said, "It is all fine that they are so happy. Only I know how hard it is going to be to conduct this wedding. It is going to kill me trying to get money from this man." (She was referring to my father.) Appa usually gave us a pittance to spend. Meena and I used to discuss that even though Manni was so frugal, he was constantly calculating the expenses. Appa's aunt told him gently, "Do not make it so difficult for Lakshmi (that was Manni's name, she was also called Ammalu in her maternal home). She cannot come to you for each wedding expense. She is clever and will provide you with a complete accounting for every paisa she spends, so give her a lump sum." It was only after hearing this that he gave Manni a reasonable sum for the wedding expenses. I am not sure how much that was.

There were many friends and relatives who came for the wedding from Vadiveeswaram to Karamanai. They were put up at a small house that belonged to one of Appa's friends. Apparently Seethai commented that it was a disgrace that they were given such inadequate accommodations. In those days the wedding ceremonies usually went on for four days. The afternoon of the fourth day was when the groom's family usually left with packaged food, vegetables, coconuts and such, provided by the bride's family. My wedding took five days. My in-laws apparently belonged to a particular sect called Godhaniar—I still do not know what that means—and that is the reason they wanted the ceremonies to last for five days. I remember a particular wedding ritual special to the Godhaniars called "fishing," where they throw a green plantain (supposed to represent a fish) into the river and have the groom pretend to fish and pick it out of the water with his shawl.

Maybe the Brahmins arrived in South India from the north and brought along with them the *Vedas*, as well as different customs, rituals and the caste system. Brahmins had to follow some extra rules as they were considered the upper caste with special privileges. There was caste gradation and with each lower caste, there was less social standing and prestige. People of the lowest caste were considered the Untouchables. This has changed a lot over the years, but I do not think it has completely disappeared. The cause for many communal clashes today is this distinction between upper and lower castes. This is so ingrained in the social structure that it is going to be hard to ever get rid of it completely.

The wedding ceremony included all the usual Brahmin customs and the special requirements for the Godhaniars (and here I wonder if they considered themselves an elite class of Brahmins) and after the wedding, the groom's entire family left with the food and snacks provided by my parents. Usually, in the four-day wedding, nothing much happens on the first day after the *Muhoortam*, initiation of the rituals at the auspicious moment in the evening. The *Nalangu* ceremony is held in the afternoons of days 2 and 3 when the groom and bride play games and people from both the families sing playful songs teasing the groom, the bride and their family members. Later in the evening after dinner on the third day there is *Sathir*, where the bride and groom sit in chairs and there is a music recital. The musician does not have to be a good one. However, wealthy people bring famous musicians. The groom's party usually leaves by the afternoon of the fourth day.

There is one function on the third day where the bride and groom sit on a wooden plank in a swing. The priest would light a fire in a pot containing cow dung, hay and wood shavings, and recite some prayers. The bridesmaids would tie a knot between the sari end of the bride and the corner of the shawl of the groom. Then the priest would ask the groom to keep a black dot on the bride's forehead. The girls would playfully knock together the heads of the bride and the groom. As the groom was keeping the black dot on my forehead one of the girls remarked, "The black dot won't even show on the groom." The other girls snickered on hearing this. I felt somewhat sad when I heard that cutting remark. The day before the wedding, my father's cousin, his uncle's daughter, had come over to me and said, "If anyone comments about the boy being dark-skinned do not take it to heart. You are lucky to have an alliance like this. You will be bedecked with jewellery from head to toe. You will have beautiful saris to wear. The groom is a lawyer, so clients will bring gifts, jackfruit, mangoes, plantains..." She had gone on and on in this vein.

During the engagement ceremony on the day before the main wedding ceremony, I did not set eyes on my husband to be. I stayed with my head bowed, looking at the floor, modestly as was expected, the entire time. I was very scared. I first had a brief look at him only during the ceremony of exchanging garlands. I knew he was somewhat dark but did not expect this kind of extreme dark complexion, and was somewhat sad about it. On the first day of the wedding, after the rituals, we (me, my husband, his parents, sister and her husband) went in a taxi to Vadiveeswaram for the formal *Grihapravesam* ceremony of the bride entering the husband's family house for the first time. Before entering the house some rituals were going on and I heard someone say at the back, "The girl looks like a painted portrait. Just the right size; not too fat, not too tall. She is beautiful. Chidambaram (referring to my husband) is lucky."

Once we entered their house, they gave us milk and fruits. My husband would occasionally turn to sneak a peek at me. I knew about this only through Manni, who described it later. I was consumed with fear thinking about the strange new surroundings, new people and also because I had heard that my sisters-in-law were not that easy to get along with. I also felt sad again. The atmosphere of the house, the way they spoke, I did not like any of that. The only positive thing was that their house was nicer and bigger than where I came from. I felt that their house was the best on the entire street. The main hall was huge and had an inner courtyard, open to the skies with a large verandah. The kitchen was spacious. There was a capacious passage. Besides, there were two separate storerooms. Most of the provisions and vessels were stored in one of those rooms called *pavul*; some of the vessels were stored beneath the staircase and this crawl space had its own door. We did not have stainless steel vessels in those days.

As part of the *Grihapravesam*, we also visited another house, which belonged to my father-in-law's brother. His wife was terminally ill. We paid our respects to her. She then raised her hand and indicated something to a person standing nearby, who then brought some money and gave it to her to hold in her hand. We bowed to her and accepted the money. (I don't remember how much it was.) I thought I saw her smile, but she also had tears in her eyes. We got the news that she passed away that night. Only later I learned that the person who brought her the money was her husband, my father-in-law's elder brother.

Since she had passed away, half of the groom's party who had come from Vadiveeswaram to Karamanai left after the first day of the wedding. On the second day we had the *nalangu* ceremony. My sisters-in-law had heard that I sang well. In our village people used to be full of praise for my looks and also my singing. I sang *Nagumomu Ganaleni*.[4] But I was so afraid that I could not sing well. Even I could make out I was going off-tune and I stopped halfway.

One of my husband's friends then said, "Chidambaram, ask her to sing another song. She will get over her nervousness then."

So he told me, "Sing '*Kamalaambaam Bhajare*.'[5] Don't be afraid."

I said, "I don't know that song," and kept quiet. For the *Sadir* function the next day, we had a musical performance by my music teacher and the day after that someone else sang, nothing extraordinary. On the fourth day of

---

[4] A composition of saint poet Thyagaraja on Rama.
[5] A composition of Muthuswami Dikshitar.

the wedding, during dinner, they had a play with people throwing coloured water at each other. On the fifth day as the in-laws were getting ready to leave, apparently my father-in-law told my sister-in-law, "Why don't we take her with us now? There is filaria in this place. She will be better off coming with us." I do not know what my sister-in-law answered but someone who heard him say that, reported it to Manni. During the wedding my sister-in-law complained about many things, but Manni never backed down. Manni kept reminding her that she had already explained that we did not have the means to meet all the demands and that even the current ceremony was a big financial stress.

After my in-laws left, ultimately everyone including our close relatives left, and then Meena and Manni started cleaning the house. It took several days to get the house back in shape. In the meantime, Appa yelled at Manni. He again said the expenses were too much. She replied, "If we want an alliance with a good family, there will be costs. As a matter of fact, I have managed to cut down expenses all around, in all sorts of ways. I did not even buy a sari for the bride. My four brothers together had gifted a sari and that is the one I passed off as our sari for the bride."

Appa was still angry. He said, "Only the person who earns will know the pain," and stormed out.

In those days silk saris were relatively inexpensive. For just fifty rupees one could buy a silk sari with a gold braid border. My four uncles pitched in and together had bought me a silk sari with a thin gold border. My in-laws gave me two saris for specific wedding ceremonies, the *Muhurtam*, the main ceremony, and *Nichayathartham*, the engagement ceremony. Usually, the in-laws are supposed to give only one sari but it was my sister-in-law's idea— she felt it was better to get two saris, each with less gold embroidery, than one expensive sari. So altogether, I got three saris for my wedding. All of them were the traditional nine-yard saris, not the more modern six-yard saris. We were all quite pleased with the bonanza!

****

Coming of Age, Husband's Illness and Some Thoughts on Widows

Within a month of our wedding, my husband was diagnosed with tuberculosis and went for rest and treatment to Madhanapalli with my sister-in-law and her husband. They stayed there for a whole year. In those days people who could afford it went to Madhanapalli, which was a sanatorium for the treatment of Tuberculosis (TB). Both in my marital family and my natal family, everyone was devastated by the news. The neighbours started visiting, seemingly to commiserate and console. These awful people would say, "Seems like the groom's family hid the serious illness and got him married. What kind of people are they?" Honestly, I do not believe my father-in-law or others knew that my husband had this disease. They had thought it was some non-specific fever, which apparently would come and go. They ultimately went to Madras and had him tested, which is when they found out it was TB. Immediately they made arrangements to go to Madhanapalli. They were there for about a year.

I started my periods six months after the wedding. In accordance with the then prevailing custom, the occasion was celebrated with great fanfare. For the main event on the third day, men and women from the husband's house usually attended, along with a few neighbours. They would be fed and then they would give money to the young girls who were also usually present, providing company to the girl who has attained menarche. It was customary to invite five to six young pre-pubertal girls (usually ten-year olds) from the neighbourhood and have them stay for three days with the girl who had come of age. They were called "Girls in Residence." They were given money and were well taken care of. They got good meals and snacks. Even I have participated in this event when I was ten. It used to be fun—plenty of snacks and also some money. In return, the girls would keep company and play all kinds of indoor games with cowrie shells with the girl who had come of age. Also, they did not have to attend school—the argument always was that it was okay if girls missed two or three days of school. These young girls would sing very raunchy songs describing intimate acts between the girl who had attained puberty and her husband.

The songs were quite explicit and vulgar. I feel rather ashamed to elaborate. The adults wrote the songs but there was no way the girls who sang the songs would not have understood the meanings. A typical song described the different ways the man enjoys the woman's body. It never mentioned anything about how a woman could enjoy the man's physique and seemed to imply that the woman was created for the man's pleasure. In those days, men considered women as objects that existed solely to satisfy their desires. The women seemed to consider it their duty to fulfil the man's lust. That resulted in the women giving birth to many children, one after the other in rapid succession. Their whole life's mission seemed to be to live for their husbands. In *Puranas* you encounter men marrying several women. Even the gods are each depicted as having more than one wife. No other religion depicts divinity in such a derogatory fashion. In the Hindu religion, on the one hand, they describe god as something/someone with no designated form or feature who is everything and nothing, omnipresent. But on the other hand, gods are described as men with emotions like anger, love and all the other desires of ordinary human beings, who also marry and have children. Worshippers treat gods like ordinary human beings by making offerings to them, in return expecting help with their own needs and desires. I feel such acts diminish the divine. Or maybe I do not get the inner meaning of it all. What I consider as degradation may be considered noble by others.

Then you have this terrible custom of ill-treating widows, which seems to be more prevalent among Hindus. At one time they burned the widows alive along with the corpses of their husbands. Thanks to the social reformer Raja Ram Mohan Roy, that custom was abolished and made illegal. However, even today it seems to be happening in some remote villages of Rajasthan. The result seems to be that instead of burning them alive, widows are destroyed in every possible way. Like I have said earlier, their jewels and auspicious symbols are taken away and they have to remain indoors in a white sari for a year. They can't even visit close relatives for a year. I have already written about how the status of widows has improved in the present times. I continue to harp on this subject because I want to emphasize that a woman is not in any way inferior to a man. If there is no woman there will be no man either. Women are as much emotional beings as men. I also believe that women are more intelligent than men but they are treated like inanimate objects.

Among Brahmins, there were young girls who were widowed by the time they were five to seven years old. When a child widow attained puberty, the parents would shave her hair and keep her indoors. I have seen such women. The famous writer Kalki had written a story graphically describing this injustice. I enjoyed reading Kalki's stories and essays. He was a great writer and was one of the eminent personalities who fought for independence from the British. He wrote extensively on various flawed social practices like untouchability, superstitions, child marriage and the plight of widows. He wrote with an element of biting sarcasm, and he would make you think and empathize.

Widows were not allowed to participate in festive celebrations, but they were always in the background toiling to make all the sweets and other eatables. In those days whenever there was a wedding, there would be at least four or five young widows in the back patio, the most remote end of the house, who would have been assigned to do some work or the other. They were unpaid labourers. However, they did their work happily as that seemed to be the only social outlet for them.

I never used to pay much attention to the plight of these widows, until the time I had a certain conversation with my friend Avadai. She was two years older than me. She had been married for two years when this conversation occurred. She visited me at my house in Karamanai and said, "I heard your husband has TB, now that is a terrible disease and very few people survive. My mother says that only your luck and the strength of your wedding pendant (*thali*) will help him overcome this. You look gorgeous like a statue made of gold. Hope your husband can beat this. Otherwise, your life is finished." She continued, rattling away in a blend of Malayalam and Tamil,[6] "They will ban you from wearing any jewellery, they will not allow you to apply turmeric, no flowers for you, even your thick black hair will be gone. You will most likely have to wear a white sari..." And she went on and on.

Manni was taking a nap in the corridor and when she heard this, she jumped up, came to us and yelled at Avadai, "What kind of nonsense are you talking to this child? How can a young girl like you talk like this? If I could, I would cut your tongue for speaking such awful things. Don't ever come to our house again. As it is we are worried sick. Only Nataraja (Thatha's god, our family deity) can help. Nothing will happen to that boy (my husband). Nataraja will take care..."

I visited Avadai several years later and remembered that she had caused me to become extremely anxious after the conversation that we had during the time my husband was ill. Any time I saw a tonsured person I would start thinking about my situation and feared I would have to have my head tonsured if my husband died. I could not

---

[6] Tamilians in Thiruvananthapuram spoke a mixed dialect.

bear to think of that possibility; I would be overwhelmed with fear and start crying. I began to feel empathy for all widows—old or young. However, from what I see, most people do not seem to be too bothered about this social ill. Even my older daughter, who was into women's rights and was always proclaiming that men were controlling women, did not seem to be bothered a whole lot about the plight of widows. I don't know why this issue bothers me so much. In my opinion, even today, society does not seem to embrace widows wholeheartedly. I always wondered why the issues faced by widows bothered me this much and it is possible that my friend Avadai's words deeply affected me. There is a saying that you realize or understand adversity only when you are personally affected—that is absolutely true!

While I think that it is only among Hindus that widows are mistreated so much, my children disagree. Once, I had a very intense argument with my older son regarding this issue that almost turned into a confrontation. We were talking about the famous playback singer Janaki. I saw her being interviewed on TV, wearing the traditional widow's white sari, and I was shocked and saddened. She had recently lost her husband. I turned to my son who was also watching the show and said, "It is awful that she has to appear like this in a white sari and a bare forehead without a *pottu* and not a single piece of jewellery in this day and age."

My son did not seem to be affected by the spectacle. He replied, "She has chosen to do this to herself. Nobody is responsible for this and they can't be either. It is only in the Hindu religion that one has a choice of going to the temple or not. In other faiths, they are forced to go to their temples. In the Muslim religion, women are ill-treated. They cannot go out freely. The men can each customarily marry up to four women, and their laws and religion allow it. Also, simply by saying 'talaq' three times, they can divorce a wife. They do not have to give alimony. Their women do not even have the freedom to apply nail polish. Recently a woman's finger was cut off as a punishment for applying nail polish. You are always against the Hindu religion…"And so he went on and on and shut me up. My older daughter has also spoken to me many times about the mistreatment of women among Muslims, and I have to admit that even I have read about such mistreatment in the magazines.

After that, I saw Janaki in several interviews on TV. Every time I saw her, I got irritated. She has not remained hidden indoors after her husband's death. She participated in all social functions, continued to be a playback singer in several languages, and generally seemed very happy. And that is the way she should be too. However, I could not understand why she still appeared in widow's garments. I brought up this issue once again when I shared my thoughts with my son and he said, "That is what I mean. This is not a requirement imposed by the Hindu religion. You and aunties Pappa and Seethai did not follow the old traditions…" He also gave examples of so many others. "You have remained the way you were [before widowhood]. Can't you make out from this? This shows that even early on, some brave women, possibly educated women, broke away from tradition and then others followed and the custom of widows wearing white saris faded. The same goes for Brahmin widows tonsuring their heads."

"It was probably due to social pressures that they put up with these customs...," I said.

"Those days are gone. I repeat, it is totally Janaki's choice that she is doing this now. Nobody would have forced her..." My son said.

There is no point arguing with him. My son and daughter are well educated; they will not take the words of a simple person like me seriously. After all, for years my in-laws, especially my two sisters-in-law, have called me stupid and referred to me that way when talking about me to my older children as well as to the whole family and our neighbours in the street. They have been doing it for years. There was a time when my older sister-in-law Seethai was like an all-powerful dictator in the Palla Street neighbourhood where she lived. These people have a herd mentality. I have been an insignificant person in my household. Given this, who would take my views seriously? With these thoughts flowing in my mind I decided not to continue the dialogue with my son. But I felt that I should somehow express my thoughts and so let me continue this chronicle from where I left off.

I feel Janaki conformed to the old tradition because of her superstitious belief that if widows do not adhere to certain rules, their deceased husbands would meet with distress in the nether world. Also, Janaki may have thought that since she is a well-known singer and a public figure she would be respected only if she played the role of a widow. Since she, for some reason, believed in those superstitious Hindu customs and followed them, I will definitely place the blame, for Janaki opting to appear as if she were a dead tree, on the Hindu religion. Where India is concerned, I agree that other religions, especially Islam, have some draconian rules for women. But I have chosen to voice my opinion only about the terrible injustice done to Hindu widows. I am not against the Hindu religion, but I want to purge blind beliefs from the religion and retain only the good and noble parts. However people take it, I have just vented my concerns. I feel that the topic of Hindu widows is an important one that needed to be a part of my autobiography.

What my friend Avadai predicted did not happen. My husband lived to the ripe old age of 80 before he passed away. For the most part, he remained very healthy. I attained puberty within six months of his going to Madhanapalli for treatment of TB. We kept receiving news about him slowly recovering from his illness. Around the time I came of age, he had recovered almost completely. So, the celebratory function for coming of age (I don't really want to write about it at this point in time but I have to say it as it happened even if it seems unrefined) was celebrated with a grand function in our house. Since my husband was at Madhanapalli for almost a year after our wedding, we did not have any occasion to celebrate and give the traditional gifts during that year to our in-laws. In those days, the gifts, especially sweets and snacks, were given from the bride's house to the bridegroom's for festivals throughout the year for the festivals of Avani Avittam, where men wear a new sacred thread and discard the older one to signify a new beginning, Kaarthikai, the festival of lighted lamps, Pongal, the harvest festival, etc.

The mother accompanied by her daughter would go to the groom's place with the gifts if they happened to live nearby. If that is not convenient for the mother for some reason, the girl would be sent with some close relative to the groom's house. Normally the gifts would be taken only by women. This made it convenient for the mother-in-law, sisters-in-law and others to find fault with whatever was brought. For Deepavali, the groom would come with his family to the bride's place. Since my husband was ill, we did not have to come up with the gold waist chain that we had agreed to gift during Deepavali to the groom.

At this juncture, I do have to praise my sister-in-law Seethai for the care she provided to my husband, her younger brother. She took exceptional care of him during the time he was ill, and made sure he got nourishing food and the medications prescribed by the doctor. The praise extends to her husband too. He was extremely affectionate and treated my husband as his own brother. Seethai showed a lot of affection towards her stepbrothers too, but my husband had a special place in her heart. She was also very fond of my oldest daughter Shobha (Subbalaxmi), the first girl to be born after a long void in the family. Also, my daughter was very fair and plump when she was a baby. Maybe Seethai was attracted to Shobha's looks.

Both Seethai and her husband spent the whole year in Madhanapalli while my husband recovered from his illness. Even after returning to Vadiveeswaram, they spent another year in Ramavarmapuram, a suburb of Nagercoil, in a rented house. That part of the town was breezy. The house had a compound with plenty of plants and trees whereas in our village, Vadiveeswaram, the houses were next to each other and cramped, and there was less hygiene. Since the doctor had advised that he should be in a place where he can breathe fresh air, they decided to move to this place. The interesting part is that these two neighbourhoods were not all that far away from each other, maybe a mile or two. At that time, there were very few houses in Ramavarmapuram. Most houses had a compound and there were so many jackfruit, mango, coconut trees around that it was a treat to the eyes. Even at the height of summer, you did not feel the heat.

Manni prepared the sweets and snacks that were due for the festival of Karthikai and took me to my in-laws' place in Vadiveeswaram. We lit the lamps for Karthikai along with my husband's younger sister Pappa and the stepmother whom everyone called Chithi. Two days later Manni and I went back to Karamanai. We returned in two months at the time of Pongal, the harvest festival. At the request of my sister-in-law, Manni and Appa (whom we called Anna, elder brother) left me behind. Appa had come specially to meet my husband. I stayed with them for ten days in the Ramavarmapuram house. My husband had gained weight. He was resting most of the time. When no one was around, he tried on many occasions to speak to me. I would usually find a way to run away. At the same time, I *did* want to be near him and see him. For him to enjoy the breeze, they had placed a cot on the patio. He would usually rest there. It was then that on two occasions, without his knowledge, I hid and had a good look at him and thought to myself: He has thick black hair and looks healthier than he did during the wedding. Also, he doesn't seem as dark as he did during the wedding. He is an educated person too... and reassured myself.

One day his childhood friend Raman came. Raman asked, "What's up, Chidambaram, did you talk to your wife?"

My husband replied, "Nothing much has happened; she just runs away every time I try to talk to her."

Raman said, "She is very young and new to all this. It will all work out as time goes by." My husband just smiled.

I was taken by the Ramavarmapuram house and the garden surrounding it. It was so idyllic that I wished they would stay there forever. They were planning to go back to Vadiveeswaram anytime. The Vadiveeswaram house was okay but I did not like the neighbourhood. In two months would be the nuptials ceremony. They were supposed to go back to Vadiveeswaram before that. That thought made me sad. Meanwhile, sister-in-law Seethai and her husband had to attend a family function in Thiruvananthapuram. They took me along. That was the second time since my wedding that my sister-in-law came to visit our house in Karamanai. She did not stay too long and spoke very little. Maybe she was upset that all the formal celebrations following the wedding, which required the bride's family to bring gifts to the groom's house for festivals during the first year, could not happen. Even the second Deepavali celebration did not take place as the doctors had restricted travel for my husband. In any case, my sister-in-law never seemed to like my family. She did not feel that we were good enough for their family. She has told me so on many occasions.

Let me elaborate. Seethai would say, "Chithi is not well (she had epilepsy); I thought this girl (referring to me) from a large family could help with household chores.

Pappa (younger sister) can't be here always. If her husband gets a job she will have to go with him. I thought she, as the daughter-in-law, could take care of Chithi. Even though their family is not up to our standards, since the girl was good looking I arranged the match. Her mother is a very smart woman. I thought her mother would have taught her how to work in the kitchen. On the contrary, she doesn't know a thing..." Seethai would go on like this all the time to people visiting the house during the early days when I had begun to live there.

Some of the visitors would say, "She is still a child. She will learn as time goes by."

Seethai would retort, "By the time I was ten I could make the *murukku* and sweet balls. I could easily grind a large quantity of rice in a minute. My sister Pappa could cook by the time she was 12; she would grind daily for *dosai*, and she could do everything quickly and efficiently."

Actually what Seethai said was true. At our house, my older sister took care of everything, and she wouldn't let me do anything in the kitchen. I would fetch the water from the river, draw water from the well, sweep the floor and draw the *kolam* at the threshold. But I never went near the kitchen stove. If anyone asked if I could sing Seethai would quickly say I could not sing based on my nervous attempt to sing during the wedding. The people of Vadiveeswaram village were convinced by her and considered me a dumb, good-for-nothing individual. Seethai continued to insult me until the time my older daughter got married. I will write in detail about how she hurt me later.

****

My Married Life in Vadiveeswaram

When Shanti Kalyanam, or nuptial ceremony to officially consummate the marriage, happened, I was not yet 16. The stay in Ramavarmapuram had made me feel some love and respect towards my husband. Manni managed to come up with gifts for the Shanti Kalyanam from what she had received from her parental family for her own Shanti Kalyanam—a bed, large mirror, a round table with chair, some vessels, sweets and other snacks, a silk dhoti for the son-in-law, two silk saris for me (one with a good amount of brocade and the other a simple one), etc. We still have that bed, table and mirror in our house. The bed was, however, just wide enough for one person to lie down comfortably. During my Shanti Kalyanam ceremony, my mother was pregnant with my youngest sister Krishna. I think she was six or seven months pregnant. Of course, my sister-in-law did comment: "At 40, with a grandchild, here is the bride's mother having yet another child of her own!"

In those days, during the nuptial ceremony, the mothers usually advised the daughters to accept, bear and go along with whatever the husband did. My mother did the same. Maybe the erotic songs the elders taught the little girls to sing during the menarche ceremony were to educate and prepare the girl.

On that first night, my husband asked me, "I really like you a lot. Do you like me?"

I just mumbled, "Mmm."

My husband kept talking, "My friend Ramaswami told me about you. He told me you are a classy girl and I am one lucky guy." My husband liked good music, tasty food, good cinema, books, his cigarettes and drinks. Actually, just a couple of cigarettes a day and an occasional drink when he had good company. He also liked sex. It was different for me. I enjoyed it until I was 40 years old. After that, I completely lost interest in sex. Maybe if I had started writing my autobiography at a very young age I would have talked in more detail about sex as an experience.

The Ramaswami he mentioned was the son of one of the disciples of my grandfather. His family used to attend all the religious functions conducted by my grandfather. My grandfather had spoken to their family about a possible alliance between Ramaswami and me. Whenever Ramaswami came, my cousin, my older maternal aunt's son, would tease me saying, "Your husband is here, go and hide." Since the girls got married at a very young age, it was quite usual for them to run away and hide when the husband showed up. I was 10 or 11 years old then and my cousin was 25. He was staying at my grandfather's place and trying to finish his BA. He was not all that good with his studies. He kept at it, clearing one exam at a time and somehow completed his BA. As soon as Ramaswami stepped inside the house, my cousin would start teasing me and I would cry. He enjoyed that. I did not like Ramaswami at all, despite him being quite good looking. Seeing me cry he would tell my cousin, "She is a child. Why are you bullying her?"

My husband knew Ramaswami well but not as a close friend. My husband had four very close friends. One of them was Sundaram, who visited often. He lived in the next town and his conversations always revolved around sex. He liked looking at women, inspecting them from head to toe, especially their breasts. He was very much into music. He was very knowledgeable, and also sang but did not have a good voice. He came from a family of musicians. His family did not have a good reputation as far as their dealings with women were concerned. I used to ask my husband why Sundaram constantly commented about women saying, "This woman is like so and so; that other woman is different. Her face is beautiful but everything else is no good. The girl across the street is perfect, just like a statue. How sculpted her breasts look!" And so on. My husband himself had told me about such comments of Sundaram. Others had also told me about him. My husband's take on this was, "He is just frank about his opinions. Others may think in the same way but may not voice it. You don't know men, in fact, you do not know much about women either. In general, girls don't express themselves as openly as boys do." I did not have the guts to talk back to him in those days, although I did not always agree with everything he said.

There is one thing I must mention here. During that time, it was rumoured that on every street in

Vadiveeswaram, at least one or two women had extra-marital affairs. I used to disapprove of these women but as time passed by I felt differently about this issue. Ninety per cent of the men seemed to misbehave in their relationships with women, and society seemed to tolerate this, but if an occasional woman gives in to desire, society treats them very harshly. She is called wayward and a prostitute. In fact, such labels are given by other women. Women seem to relish calling another woman characterless. It is very true that women are their own worst enemies.

Women would very often say, "He is a man after all," and would condone misbehaviours of a man. I have heard this being said more often by women than men. Occasionally when a widower decides not to remarry, his mother and sisters would attempt to persuade him to change his decision. They would say, "You need someone to take care of the house and children (it does not matter how many children he had with the first wife), and also take care of you as you age and get sick." Everything always revolved around the man's needs. On the other hand, a young widow's needs were usually ignored. Though women enforced all the customs about widows that I talked about before, I strongly believe that it was the men who made those ideas take root in society. Enslavement of women is similar to the entrenched customs related to the caste system. Such thoughts came up in my mind often.

My husband in general was a good man. He treated me with love. Like most men he too had some weaknesses. But he was very honest with me. He never spoke ill of anyone. He was always quick to praise the good qualities of others. If anyone offended him he never took it to heart, and he did not believe in brooding. He would say that one has to move on and do what has to be done. He was the best among all my in-laws. Despite that, what has always bothered me was that he was indifferent towards what was happening in my life. If there was a conflict in the house between others in the house and myself, he stayed out of it as though it never happened. I came into his house when I was not yet 16 with a lot of expectations. Unlike what everyone said would happen, the people in this family did not buy me clothes or jewellery. Even when clients came with gifts like mangoes, jackfruit, plantains, bananas, etc., I never felt free to take what I pleased. I ate the fruits only when Chithi gave them to me, and she was never generous when she offered them to me. She would offer so much more to other friends and neighbours. If Pappa came and offered something to me, Chithi would say, "I have already given her." Chithi was not a bad person. However, she was somewhat scared of my sister-in-law Seethai, and she did not think much of me. She was fond of my second sister-in-law Pappa and treated her like her own daughter.

At the time of my wedding, Pappa had been married for three years. By the time I went to live with my in-laws she had been married for four-plus years but continued to live in her parental home. Her in-laws' house was about 40 km away. Apparently, her sister-in-law and mother-in-law ill-treated her and so she was rarely sent to her marital home. And within a short while of sending her there, she would be brought back also. Since Chithi had epilepsy, she wasn't allowed to go near the stove and Pappa did all the cooking. Initially, I helped grind for the *kozhambu*, the tamarind and lentil sauce, and cleaned the plates. I began sweeping the kitchen floor every other day but soon it became a daily job. Not just that. Within a year I started doing the cooking. The main reason for that was Chithi. She would tell Pappa, "You take time off and go out. She (referring to me) and I will manage everything." At times Chithi would endearingly call Pappa "child."

In my own home, I had done other things but had never gone near the cooking stove. But Chithi started involving me in cooking slowly and managed to make me cook daily. Pappa was a good cook. She also worked efficiently in the kitchen. Grinding for *dosai* had to be done every other day. *Dosai* or *idli* was served every day at 2 p.m. for tiffin. At times we had outside help to grind for the *dosai*. Other days Pappa would do the job by 10 in the morning. She was neat with any job she did. She also washed her face four or five times a day. When she worked, she was never pleasant; she always seemed angry and used to slam the vessels. She became all smiles only when I started cooking. To keep her happy, Chithi made me share the grinding for the *dosai* which meant grinding half the quantity of rice. This was a job I had no experience with and I found it very difficult. As time went by, I got more used to it and it did not seem as tough.

Chithi never viewed me as a child and always treated me like a grown-up person. For example, when there were functions or festivals celebrated in our neighbouring houses (most of the houses in the adjoining three streets had friends or relatives), the neighbours would distribute sweets and snacks individually to every house. When these eatables came to our house, Chithi would be the one to make them into portions and distribute them. If there wasn't enough for everyone, she would not give me any, but she would also not take her own portion. Since Pappa loved eating a variety of such snacks, Chithi would give her extra.

On one such occasion when my husband was around, Pappa had her portion and there wasn't enough for everyone else, so Pappa asked, "Don't you people want any?"

Chithi answered, "All of you can have. She (referring to me) and I do not want any; we are happy seeing all of you enjoy eating it."

Then my husband said, "You can only speak for yourself. You cannot include everyone else." He was obviously referring to me.

Chithi retorted with a smirk, "Okay, then I will not do that." However, after that incident, a couple of times she did start giving me some sweets, but a smaller portion than the others. As time passed, she reverted to excluding me. Maybe old habits die hard. What can be inferred from all this is while she considered Pappa a child she did not think of me as one. The strange thing is that Pappa was five years older than me and looked older because she was also obese. The only reason I can think of for this kind of treatment is that Chithi felt that I did not belong there and I was from a different house.

In a certain way, Pappa bonded well with Chithi; she could sense that Chithi was going to have a seizure before it happened. Even I started recognizing the signs. Chithi would get incoherent in her talking and then would just fall. During those episodes, Pappa would catch hold of Chithi and gently lay her on the floor. Chithi would froth from the mouth. Pappa would wipe her clean and would wait for Chithi to regain consciousness. After that, for the rest of the day, she would let Chithi rest and not allow her to do any household work. This may be the major reason for Chithi's affection towards Pappa.

Pappa would usually finish the morning chores, have her meals, wash her face, straighten her nine-yard sari and then go to her older sister Seethai's house on the next street, the Palla Street. She would go there about 10 in the morning and return around 2 or 2:30 p.m. On some days if her sister would have prepared any of her favourite snacks, she would have tiffin at her sister's place. In the afternoon it was either Chithi or me who would make the *dosais*. At that time, I was not very good with making the *dosais* and Chithi would ask me to step aside and take over the *dosai* making task. She would usually also make three *dosais* for Pappa. She would report my incompetence in *dosai* making to Pappa and both of them would discuss this in great detail. In general, Pappa also reported every event in detail to her older sister Seethai. At times there would be small misunderstandings between Chithi and Pappa. Pappa would immediately report the minor conflict to Seethai, who would instantly come by to fight on Pappa's behalf; Chithi would give in right away. Seethai was capable of making a mountain out of a mole hill. In those days Seethai wore metal toe rings and you could hear the sound even before she appeared on our doorstep. As soon as I heard the sound I would cower with fear. Whenever there was a fight, Seethai would bring up the fact that her mother had died and she was motherless. I think she mentioned that till she was almost 50 years old.

She would come by at least twice a day to talk to her father and check me out. She would tell Chithi, "Teach her housework." I would think to myself: You do not really need to say that. Chithi is already taking me to task.

Every day from *our* house (I don't like saying that actually. No one even considered me a human being in that house. So I am going to refer to it as *that* house hereafter.) Seethai would take cooked food to her place. If Seethai did not come by, Pappa would deliver it. Not only did I not have jewellery or good clothes in that house, but I also did not even get enough food. Once in a blue moon, they used to make *murukku*. Both the sister-in-laws were good at making the *murukkus*. Seethai, especially, was an expert; she would lightly roll the dough and the *murukkus* would be so crisp.

If there was a wedding in the neighbourhood, Seethai and her cousin Periakka would go to help with the making of the *murukkus*. The wedding *murukkus* were large and both of them were good at making them. Both the cousins were also experts in making sweet cashew rolls and *kunjaladu*, both of which are very difficult to make. *Kunjaladu* has very crisp gram flour bead-balls and it needs a properly warmed up sugar syrup to be dipped into. It is not easy to roll it into big sized balls. Only they could hold it in their hands and turn them into balls. It was the same with cashew rolls. In Vadiveeswaram those days, it was customary to make *kunjaladu* and cashew rolls during weddings. Both were well known in Vadiveeswaram for their expertise in this.

Periakka was also very good at handicrafts. She could make flower garlands and embroider. She was very good at hairdos using the Thazhambu (screw pine) flower, which has to be darned into the hair. During the Ganesha festival, she would make a beautiful Ganesha out of clay. She could also make a clay oven, and people would call her to make such a special oven for them. Overall she was multitalented. The cousins were excellent at planning weddings, including the details and logistics. So everyone in the *agraharam* consulted them for the planning of any major event. Periakka was considered to be quite dominating, but unlike my sister-in-law Seethai, she did not have much time to gossip. She had many difficulties in her personal life. She spent most of her time at her younger sister's place. That sister was rather timid and she had five children. She was considered naïve, but was quite wealthy. Periakka did all the household chores including shopping. Periakka's husband was considered to be no good since he did not have a steady job. They had two sons. The older son had passed high school, learned typing and shorthand, and worked for a company in Bombay. In those days poor people, and those who were better off but did not have an aptitude or inclination for higher education, would learn typing and shorthand and would go to big cities like Bombay, Pune or Calcutta to find jobs. It was easy to get jobs for this kind of qualification. Periakka's other son was not at all smart, and I think he had only a fifth-grade education.

Periakka died of uterine cancer when she was 54. Due to a lack of proper medical treatment, she suffered towards the end. The reason why I am spending so much time describing Periakka although she was only a cousin of that house, is because she was the only person in my in-laws' family who was nice to me till the end. I still remember something she told me. When it was decided that my husband's stepmother's mother (Chithi's mother) would move into our home from Mahadanapuram, Periakka warned me that Chithi's mother could be very cruel and that she was a venomous snake. Apparently, Periakka's niece (brother's daughter) was married into Chithi's family and Chithi's mother mistreated her and ultimately caused the marriage to break up.

Periakka's brother was her stepbrother through her father's second marriage. In those days it was very common for men to get remarried very quickly after their wife's death. Many women died in childbirth. Sometimes the family would get the husband to remarry if the wife could not conceive. The parents thought nothing of getting their young daughters married to older men. Poor parents did not have any other option. A woman had no other way of earning a livelihood other than marry. Periakka's brother's daughter was a bit naïve, like me. Chithi's maternal uncle (to whom this girl was married) was a music teacher and it was with music that he earned a living. They were poor. I had seen Chithi's father once when he had come home. Later I was told that he was no more. They were sending money from this house to Chithi's mother every month. I did not know how much.

****

When Dreams Become Mirages

Now back to our joint family. Preparations were in full swing to conduct the *Poonul*, the sacred thread ceremony, for my husband's stepbrothers Ganapathy and Neelakantan. My second sister-in-law Pappa was getting ready to move to Bombay with her husband Srinivasan and their daughter after the ceremony. They said that Srinivasan had found a job in the railways in Bombay. He had found this job only five years after they got married. What exactly he was doing before that was not clear. He was from Thalapathisamudram (also known as Perumazhinji), about 35 km from Nagercoil. Srinivasan's family consisted of his mother, an older and younger sister and an older brother. His father was no more. I have no idea when he passed away. Srinivasan came to Perumazhinji from Bombay to take his wife Pappa and daughter back with him to Bombay. My husband was the one who took his sister Pappa to her husband's place. To my knowledge, Srinivasan came to our house only two times. Like I mentioned before, Pappa would rarely go to her in-law's place—she would stay there for maybe at the most two weeks. Her mother-in-law and sister-in-law were supposed to be very rude people.

That was about the time I was thinking about my in-laws. I was new to this house in Vadiveeswaram. I had heard that my sisters-in-law (especially Seethai) were not so pleasant; I used to be terrified when Seethai came by. As time went by I felt everyone in that house was my enemy. All of them could not care less about me. Those in the house included my father-in-law, his older brother, my husband's stepmother (Chithi), her mother (Paatti, she came to live in the house when I was six months pregnant with my second child), my husband, his younger sister Pappa, husband's younger brother, and the three stepbrothers, sons born to Chithi. My older sister-in-law Seethai, her husband Natarajan and their son lived on the next street. Seethai used to come to our house about four or five times a day. When I arrived in this house in Vadiveeswaram, Chithi's youngest son was five years old. All the children including Seethai's son were quite fond of me.

After the *Poonul* ceremony for the stepbrothers, Ganapathi and Neelakantan, Pappa got ready to leave for Bombay. In fact, Chithi's mother was to move to our house only after Pappa left. So there was going to be one more person in the house to harass me. Periakka's warning about Paatti and her cruel nature was on my mind. The older sister Seethai did not want Chithi's mother, reputed to be a nasty woman, to come till Pappa left as she felt she would make life hard for Pappa. Everyone in the house, especially my father-in-law, Chattai, abided by his elder daughter's rules. After Pappa left, it was felt they needed someone to take care of Chithi (due to her issues with seizures), and they thought that her mother would be her best caregiver. They were already providing money for her day-to-day living. Also, Chithi was her only child. Just before the *Poonul* function someone went to Mahadhanapuram and brought Chithi's mother (she was referred to as Paatti) to Vadiveeswaram. The consensus was that no one should create any trouble for Pappa; she was the daughter of the house, whereas I was, after all, the daughter-in-law. It would not matter how I would be treated by her. The other logical reason for bringing Paatti, that Seethai emphasized, was that I was a young girl who would not know how to handle Chithi's epilepsy seizures. And Paatti being there would be helpful to me and it was, in a way, for my own good. "Be careful," Seethai advised me in a solicitous manner.

The *Poonul* was a grand function. I do not know how many clothes they bought and who they were for. They definitely did not buy me anything. Paatti was quite nice to me in the beginning. She would say, "You seem timid like my daughter. You look beautiful too. The two girls in this house are difficult people. They harass my daughter. I am poor. That is the reason I got my daughter married to this man with four children. Your parents must be reasonably well to do. You look like a painted portrait. How did you get married into this family?"

I replied, "I did what my parents told me. They did not consult me. I did not have any specific desire to get married. I must listen to my parents, isn't it? I didn't even see him (my husband) before the wedding."

At this Paatti said, "Chidambaram is very smart, he is well educated. Even though he is dark, he has sharp features. He will earn a lot in future. Looks don't matter for a man. He is going to make a lot of money." I felt happy to hear her say all this. I immediately started thinking about all the possibilities: He is going to be a lawyer in future, and he will not take up any other job as I thought. Once he starts earning enough I must persuade him to move out and have our own place. He seems to be affectionate. He will definitely listen to me. Once we are on our own, we can be independent and happy in our own way. I can buy nice dresses, jewellery and toys for my daughter and some good saris for myself too. I can also buy nice things for the son or daughter to be born (I was 19 then and expecting my second child). After the second child, we do not need to have more. I should be able to live as what I am and be independent and not be constantly fearful, like a slave. Thus I built my castles in the sky. But all that became mere mirages.

Paatti (Chithi's mother) slowly started displaying her true self. Usually, most women do not get along with their mothers-in-law, even if that person is the biological mother of the husband. In my case, I was the wife of the stepson, so why should there be any affection? Paatti stayed in our house most of the time. On rare occasions, she would spend a month in her grandson's house. This particular grandson, Thanu, was the oldest of the three sons Chithi had and was a talented cartoonist for the magazine *Ananda Vikatan* in Madras. He would draw cartoons of famous people. Here I want to recount an incident as Paatti related it to me. At that time, Vaidyanathan, my husband's younger (biological) brother had been married for a year. Thanu had taken Paatti with him to spend some time with him in Madras. Only a month had passed since her going there. (Vaidyanathan lived with his wife, Valli, at Thanu's place since his salary was not enough to set up his own establishment.) In that single month, Paatti and Valli had many small quarrels that exploded one day, whereupon Vaidyanathan told Thanu that he should send Paatti back as she was causing problems for Valli. So, Thanu apparently asked Paatti to leave since he felt that Valli had no option but to stay with her husband, whereas Paatti could go back to Vadiveeswaram. When Paatti heard this, she became furious and yelled that she had the right to stay in her grandson's place and it was they (Vaidyanathan and Valli) who should be the ones to leave. At this juncture, I am told that Vaidyanathan gathered her stuff and literally pushed her out of the house. Right or wrong, Vaidyanathan was known to stand by his wife through thick and thin. In the end, Valli prevailed and Paatti returned to Vadiveeswaram. I don't remember who brought her back.

As Paatti recounted these events, she cried. She cursed Valli and Vaidyanathan saying, "He bundled up my stuff and sent me back." She would narrate this story to all the visitors who came to the house and cry. For a while after this episode, she would heap praise on me and that went on for some time. She would say, "Vaidyanathan's heart is as dark as his skin. But Ambi (my husband) has a dark skin but his heart is as pure and white as fresh milk!" My husband was not as dark as Vaidyanathan though. Among the children of my husband's mother (my father-in-law's first wife), Vaidyanathan was considered the darkest. Paatti also said so. I felt sorry for Paatti when she narrated all this to me. But I did enjoy her short-lived praises for me and my husband while they lasted. Soon she went back to her usual ways. However, the worst offender, the one who spoke the harshest words, was my older sister-in-law Seethai.

Within a few months of Paatti's return I went to my birth home as I was expecting my second child. I told my mother about Paatti's coming back from Madras, and she remarked that it was one more thing that I had to deal with. No one from my birth home had attended the *Poonul* function of Ganapathy and Neelakantan. My mother said, "They haven't given you any jewellery. They haven't even given any gold to your beautiful daughter. They call themselves wealthy. Could not they have bought you some good saris? Before the wedding, that woman Kamakshi (the family friend who participated in the matchmaking) told me that they would be showering you with gold and silk. The child is almost two and they haven't even given her anything. I will go ask that Kamakshi."

I was used to Manni's tirades by this time, for every time I went home this happened. I replied, "Your son-in-law does not have any income. He has just completed his Bachelor's in law (after his MA) and has just started working in the court. If I ask him even for a simple thing like a bar of soap he would say 'I don't have an income as yet. My father has surely given me the key to the almirah but I can't spend as I want. Even if he does not ask me for accounts, I am obliged to account for what is spent.' Ultimately, with great reluctance, he would usually get me some cheap soap for my bath and to wash clothes!"

****

From Nine-Yard Sari to Six-Yard Sari and Muthu Mami

For the first four years after my marriage, Manni would buy me two saris per year. These were cheap, heavy ones, and I would wear those by alternating between them every other day. When I attended functions I would wear silk saris bought for my *Shanti Kalyanam* and other occasions. The saris were of the long nine-yard variety, worn in the typical traditional Brahmin style. I wore the traditional nine-yard sari for about nine years. I switched to wearing the much more comfortable and easy to wrap six-yard sari at the age of 23. A few women in the town had by then started changing over from the nine-yard sari to the six-yard sari, and slowly the number of women changing to the newer style increased. I always wanted to start wearing the six-yard sari but was afraid. Two houses down the street lived Muthu Mami. I used to visit her place often. She would say, "Women of your age are switching to the Telugu style of six-yard sari. Why don't you also wear six-yard saris? It will make you look younger unlike the nine-yard sari, which makes even the young girls look like old women."

Muthu Mami had three daughters and a son. Their family was from Vadiveeswaram but they had travelled to Burma seeking jobs. There were several people like them from Nagercoil in those days who had emigrated to Burma seeking employment. Many managed to save themselves and returned when World War II started. Mami's family was one of them. Mami's oldest daughter was two years younger than me. Everyone in their house was very friendly towards me. They were all dark-skinned and they seemed to be attracted by my fair skin. Though they were dark they had very sharp features and were good-looking. Mami had a good figure and a set of beautiful teeth. They were not as dark-skinned as the children of my husband's biological mother. They used the Thanakha bark and Thanakha powder to become fairer, and I think it worked some. (Thanakha bark and powder came from the Thankha tree, and Burmese women are supposed to have been using this herbal application for 2,000 years or so.) All of them dressed well. As I mentioned, they were very affectionate towards me. I enjoyed visiting them. We used to talk about cinema, music, clothes, jewellery, etc. At times we also discussed marriage and the physical part of it. Though Mami was older, she was like a friend and could openly speak about everything. Mami and her two daughters were the ones who made me switch to six-yard saris. My secret desire to wear six-yard sari was further stirred by them.

When I switched to wearing the six-yard sari, in our house they treated me like I had committed a murder. Sister-in-law Seethai said that Muthu was a bad influence on me. She would malign Muthu Mami and also me in the process saying, "She is not a good woman. With her honeyed tongue, she would cause a rift in the family. And this one (referring to me) would go and tell her all that happens at home." Muthu Mami and Seethai had been childhood friends but their friendship was a facade. When meeting in person they were very cordial, but in reality, they intensely disliked each other.

I mentioned Seethai's rants to Muthu Mami, and she said, "You should not bother and be afraid. You look young in six-yard sari. Why should you appear old at 23? They don't have good designs suitable for youngsters in the nine-yard sari styles. Come with me to the shop. We will buy two nice voile six-yard saris for you." I had saved the gift money that I had received for myself and my two children from family and friends for various functions like *Pongal* and *Karthikai*, about 1500 rupees in all, and I had put it aside as money that belonged to me. So I was able to buy two voile saris for 20 rupees. Initially, just to try out, I had worn a sari of Mami's daughter Sundari. When I wore my newly bought voile sari, Mami and her daughters said I looked very beautiful. I looked at myself in the mirror and felt I looked younger and more beautiful. But at our house everyone, except my husband, treated me like I had done something very wrong. As usual, I managed not to respond to their comments and ignore them. I used to be so afraid of them, and I really don't know how I got the courage to defy them in this particular matter. Later, I gave one of my wedding saris and the sari I was gifted during my pregnancy (both nine-yard silk saris) to Manni and got 80 rupees for those. I had asked for 100 rupees but my mother said she could only afford 80. Manni also agreed that I looked better in the six-yard sari. With that money I bought myself a simple sari without brocade in light orange colour of *kanakambaram*, the firecracker flower, with a black border and another sari in golden yellow, the colour of a gold-coloured beetle, with light gold brocade border. Muthu Mami helped me select the saris. She and her daughters praised my choice and complimented me when I wore them. In general, whenever I wore those saris I received many compliments from the neighbours also.

One day, in the night, after everyone had gone to sleep, I wore the orange-coloured sari, went upstairs and stood in front of my husband, who was deep into his books. He normally was up late till midnight every day reading. He did not even look up. Since the electricity would go off often and the bulbs were also not bright, usually he would be lying on his stomach while reading and would have a bright oil lamp next to him.

I waited for some time, then said, "Look up."

He said, "Why do you want me to look at you? Oh, I see... You have a new sari. Looks really good." Having said that he went back to his reading. I was quite disappointed and I decided then and there that I wouldn't bother to impress him anymore. I was angry but didn't say anything, and maybe it is this kind of meekness that has made other people think that they can get away with disrespecting me and has given them the temerity to insult me.

Slowly the uproar in the house about my wearing six-yard saris diminished, but they continued to harp on other issues. Paatti would tell anyone who came by how she and her daughter (referring to Chithi) were doing all the work in the house with hardly any help from me. Chithi, on her part, would tell everyone that it was her mother who was toiling in the kitchen. The truth was that I usually did the grinding for the *kozhambu*, would draw water from the well, fill the stone tank, and also fill the cement tank inside the house that could hold four pots of water. On some days I swept the kitchen floor and also helped with grinding flour for the *dosais*. When Pappa had been here we used to do the grinding on alternative days. I had learned all this after coming to my husband's house in Vadiveeswaram. It was Chithi who taught me most of the kitchen work. Since one had to bathe before cooking, Paatti started the cooking in the early morning after her bath and she also made the *dosais*. Freshly made *dosais* would be first served to my father-in-law, his brother and my husband in the early afternoon. My husband and his father returned from court around 1:30 p.m. After they ate, Paatti would make *dosais* for Chithi and me. Every time we ate, Paatti would pointedly observe that Chithi ate only two *dosais* and how she was weak and not well. Because of her daily comments, I decreased my daily *dosai* consumption from three to two.

When Paatti came to stay in this house permanently, Ganapathy and Neelakantan were in school. More *dosais* would be made and kept for them, and Paatti would finish up by making four or five *dosais* for herself. (She usually ate snacks like *dosais* at night instead of rice.) Both the brothers drank only semolina porridge for the night. The coffee we drank used to be a watered-down coffee. Milkman Sivathanu brought a pot of watered-down milk (I don't know how much it cost) every day, and Chithi would add more water to it and boil it. My daughter and son were fed this poor-quality milk as they were growing up. This would be supplemented with some finger millet porridge. As they got older, easy to digest food like ghee and lentils with rice, along with *idlis*, were added to the diet.

In those days we got our buttermilk and curd from a woman of the Yadava community who were cowherds. The butter would have been removed from it. The curd won't be thick but will not be as watery as the buttermilk. Some days the curd would be really thick and nice. It was only after my husband Chidambaram started having a steady income, the quality of the dairy products we had at home improved. The milk would be heated on slow fire until light cream floated to the surface, then after it cooled a small amount of curd would be added to it to make more curd. The next day it would be churned to remove the butter from it. We would put the curd in a bronze vessel, and add a little water. There were two chains fixed to one of the hallway pillars at two levels. The wooden churning stick was attached to these chains with the bottom end of the stick inside the curd. We would pull the chains back and forth to churn the curd. Most of the time I would do the churning and get the butter out of the curd. Over time the beautiful bronze vessel I had brought from my mother's place for churning curd got damaged and developed a leak.

****

The Emerald Chain

Let me mention two important things and later write about how I was harassed after my husband began to earn a regular income. You can consider that the second phase or chapter of my life. Every four or five months Manni or Anna (my father) used to come and take me to their place for a break. Seethai would usually ignore them when they visited. Once, when I returned after my Karamanai visit, Pappa was visiting from Bombay, and she showed me a chain with an oval-shaped emerald pendant and said, "This is in fashion now. It is only two sovereigns."

I told her it looked very nice and she said, "We have bought the emerald pendant for you too. When you go next to Karamanai ask your mother to make a chain for you with the emerald pendant. It will need just two sovereigns of gold." I was shaken. I knew that much gold would be a lot for Manni and she would definitely refuse.

The time came to visit my parental home. Someone close to the family came and took me home. With great hesitation, I told Manni about this matter. As I expected, she was furious and said, "You are not my only daughter. I am not going to give even a grain of gold. You are married and have two children now. Your in-laws have not given you even a single gold ornament, or even good clothes, and no good food either. I wonder how those people from Vadiveeswaram told us that you would be treated like family and be showered with clothes and jewellery. They are yet to give the jewel piece promised for the *Kannikadhanam*."[7] Manni went on to blast the inability of my husband to take my side and the ways of my in-laws.

I replied, "Apparently you did not pay them the full dowry amount of 2,250 rupees. You gave only 2,000 rupees. The remaining 250 rupees hasn't been given. And that is the reason they say they did not give the jewel for *Kannikadhanam*, and that is what my sister-in-law keeps telling all and sundry."

Manni then said, "Affluent people will not behave this way. Do you mean, for a mere 250 rupees they have not yet given the jewel piece all these years? Now you belong to their house. Anyway, don't keep telling me your husband is not earning anything. I am tired of hearing that."

I told her finally, "You normally have bits and pieces of gold. Even one sovereign will do."

She retorted, "Stop asking me again and again. I don't have even one bit of gold. Even if I had I will not give it to you. The jewels I have made for the common pool is for some emergency. When you are here you can wear any of the ornaments that I have; wear them as much as you want and go and attend weddings and other functions."

I then said, "I really don't want any more gold than the amount you have already given me, but if I return

____

[7] The ceremonial giving away of the bride during the wedding.

without this chain my sisters-in-law will speak very badly of you and me. They never hesitate to talk down to me. The older one will speak with anger, the younger with sarcasm."

Manni replied, "You should not meekly take all those insults."

I reminded her, "Manni, imagine you telling me this. At the time of my wedding, it was you and Paatti who advised me saying, 'Don't be rude to your in-laws, especially the sisters-in-law. Whatever they say, don't talk back. If you are patient for a while your husband will take up a job like others and go to Bombay or Calcutta. And he will have to take you along. Then you can live the way you want.' You said all this. Those words made a deep impression on me. When my in-laws badmouth us, I am fearful and resentful but am unable to come up with a suitable retort. I feel I am alone there. There is no one to support me. Chithi and her mother also usually join in the chorus. But when my sisters-in-law are not around, Paatti would say that Seethai torments her daughter the same way and that her daughter was also scared of my sisters-in-law."

After this exchange, I told Manni, "I have an extra wedding *thali*. It weighs two sovereigns. We can melt and make this chain with the emerald pendant. You can pay just the making charges."

Manni said, "Not bad, you seem to know the value of the gold you have, but if you do this and your in-laws find out they will chew you out."

I told Manni, "They will not find out and even if they do, I will stand up to them like you tell me to."

Manni then said, "They will say that I advised you in this matter. I can't hear what they say; so it won't affect me, in any case."

In due course, the goldsmith brought the chain with the emerald pendant.

Soon it was time for me to return to my in-laws' place in Vadiveeswaram. I must mention here that every time I had to leave my birth home for the hell on earth that was my in-laws' place, I would be overcome with sadness. As the journey became imminent, Meena would not let me do any work. She would make me tasty food and snacks. If it was the season for flowers, she would decorate my hair (I had beautiful long hair) with different flower arrangements. I would attend functions like weddings and celebrations for pregnant mothers in the neighbourhood, and Manni would let me wear some of the jewellery from the common pool. She would do that despite my objections. I would say that I could not wear ornaments that did not belong to me. Even though I objected, ultimately I enjoyed wearing the jewellery because I loved jewellery. I would get a special reception at the functions that I attended. It may be because of the jewels. People would enquire, "Are the gold waistband and armbands that you are wearing given to you by your in-laws?"

Manni would immediately reply (usually she accompanied me to these functions), "They have not given her even a small grain of gold. Not only that, they have given nothing for her lovely baby girl either, even though her baby is the first child of the eldest son in the family. Neither the father-in-law nor the sister-in-law felt like seeing the child with jewels and enjoy her beauty. These people are supposed to be wealthy…" Manni would go on like this and so the joy I felt wearing the jewellery was usually short-lived. As I said earlier, with all this, I usually went back to my in-laws' place with a heavy heart. It truly felt like going back to hell.

After reaching there I showed everyone my new gold chain with the emerald pendant and it was much appreciated. Six months passed. One day, as I was bathing in the local pond, the water washed away my wedding chain with its *thali*. Everyone said to look for it with a sieve, but it could not be found. In those days we wore a loose one-piece blouse (almost like a male undershirt). I think I lost the gold wedding chain and *thali* when I removed the blouse by pulling it over my head. I noticed it was gone only after reaching home. Everyone at home suggested I take out my second "extra" wedding *thali* (they knew I had two) and wear it tied to a yellow thread, considered sacred (to serve as a temporary replacement for the chain), which they would get from the priest with his blessings. My sister-in-law then went on to say, "How can you be so careless? One sovereign of gold is almost 25 rupees. How can a mother of two (I was only 23 years old though) be so careless, so irresponsible?" Stepmother and her mother joined the chorus of disapproval. Thank goodness the younger sister-in-law was not there at that time, else I would have probably got an earful of the sarcastic remarks that she was so good at making. She used to run down her own husband, that too in public. I never heard that man say anything bad about his wife. Like me he would also be quiet and never respond.

Now back to the wedding chain saga. When my sister-in-law asked for my other *thali* I was terrified. I finally had to tell the truth about using the extra gold *thali* to make a chain for the pendant. My sister-in-law said, "Oh! Your mother is shrewd. She had no qualms melting the sacred *thali* and making it. She has so much gold jewellery stashed away—chains, waistband, armband, and with all that she couldn't give two sovereigns of gold to her own daughter!"

At this point, I softly said, "Manni did not suggest using the wedding *thali*, she just said she couldn't afford to make the chain. I was the one who came up with the idea and pressurized her." As I said this, I felt quite scared.

My sister-in-law retorted, "Your mother should have advised against this. She is the daughter of a holy man and knows the customs. How could she allow you to do this? Can a mother do this for two sovereigns of gold?" She then abused me and my family and wondered from where another *thali* was going to come. At this time Chithi interceded. She said that she had a small spare wedding *thali* that I could wear with the thread for the present while my mother arranged to make a new gold chain and *thali*. Seethai completely approved and Chithi's mother was all praise for Chithi for coming up with this solution.

Here I want to reiterate that my family (Manni and Thatha) did not believe in traditions based on the *shastras* or for that matter superstitions. Thatha was a disciple of Ramalinga Swami, also known as Vallalar, who used to say that mythologies and *shastras* should not be taken as truths. Ramalinga Swami worshipped god in the abstract, as a bright glorious light. He has emphasized compas-

sion for all living creatures. He treated everyone as equal
and did not differentiate based on caste or religion. He
has firmly said that whoever follows him must believe in
non-killing or they cannot be his disciples. He also was
a proponent and practitioner of charity, providing food
for the needy. He has composed many songs in praise of
the eternal Nataraja he worshipped. He has sung them in
a way that melts one's heart. The Nataraja deity he worshipped is enshrined in Vadalur. The lamp that he lit there
apparently continues to shine. I am not sure if that is true.
I do not think he performed any miracles, and I haven't
read his life story. However, recently when the scholar
Suki Sivam spoke on TV, he described Ramalinga Swami as a revolutionary. Even today in Vadalur, Ramalinga
Swami's disciples celebrate the day he reached the state
of Samadhi when he consciously left his body, as Guru
Pooja day. Vallalar is always dressed in white. Thatha and
his family who followed Vallalar were devoted to *Arutpa*,
the book of his songs and Nataraja whom we worshipped.
As far as Manni was concerned, she did not think that
a husband's life is contained in *thali*, as people believe.
The present-day girls don't give so much importance to
thali. I have written in my memoirs about *thali* elsewhere.
But she knew that if the in-laws came to know about my
thali they would pounce on me and that Seethai, especially, would come out with some venomous words and
this worried her. When Manni had told me that Seethai
would speak harshly against not only her but also me, I
had told her that she would never come to know in any
case what was spoken about her. Manni had then said,
"Let her speak what she wants about me. But I feel sad

that you will be caught on the wrong foot and will not know how to defend yourself." Everything that happened here was exactly the way Manni had predicted. Chithi gave me the small wedding *thali* and I wore it attached to a yellow thread. Six months later Manni sent me a gold chain with a small gold *thali*, totalling four sovereigns. My in-laws commented that it was too flimsy and would break. I had to remove it every night to prevent damage, and this helped it last for seven to eight years.

Later Manni gave me a thicker double-stranded gold chain known as Goharjan chain (she was a famous singer and a kathak artiste. Those days there were saris and chains in her name sold as Goharjan sari and Goharjan chain. In fact, Arani Kuppusamy Mudaliar even wrote a novel called *Goharjan*.) and a double-stranded pearl chain. They were made with less gold. In Vadiveeswaram, the ladies wore solid heavy gold chains made with 10 to 12 sovereigns of gold. Normally the chain in which the *thali* was attached would be a heavy one. Since the one Manni gave was four sovereigns I did not wear the *thali* chain and the pearl chain daily. I wore them only on special occasions or when I attended weddings or some other function. At other times, I went back to wearing the wedding *thali* with the yellow thread instead of the gold chain. No wonder the District Collector's mother-in-law, who visited our house as a guest, thought I was the cook!

This was the mother-in-law of Bhoothalingam, who was from Vadiveeswaram, and was an Indian Civil Service (ICS) officer. My sister-in-law knew their family well, and Bhoothalingam's sister was her close friend. In those days, passing the ICS exam was a significant achievement.

(Bhoothalingam was mostly posted in Delhi after 1947 as far as I know. His wife Mathuram wrote stories in the name of "Krithika.") The mother-in-law of such a high profile person would not be a simple person. She was a very polished woman, very well-dressed in a modern way. She was about 50 years old but looked ten years younger. She saw me in my drab clothes wearing a yellow thread instead of the gold wedding chain with the *thali* and therefore assumed that I was a servant and asked if I was the cook. Lest she may ask something else, Seethai quickly replied, "She is my younger brother's wife." Since she was brought unannounced, I was in my usual clothes. The lady seemed embarrassed that she had asked such a question and tried to make up saying, "Even without jewellery and other things you are beautiful." Before she could continue, my sister-in-law whisked her away. I think she was worried I might say something inappropriate in reply. As the lady was leaving she looked at me and bid me farewell saying, "See you, my child."

Later my sister-in-law chided me and said, "You could have worn that gold chain of yours…" I said "yes" and left it at that because she spoke with me only to find faults. My sister-in-law usually spoke to me only when she had to express disapproval. After Manni sent me the double-stranded chain, I threw away the yellow thread and wore the gold chain on a daily basis. Chithi immediately took back the small *thali* that she had loaned to me. In those days that half sovereign of gold would have cost 10 rupees or so. I am mentioning this here so that the readers will come to know that these people cannot be considered well-intentioned when they would not even give half a sovereign of gold to their daughter-in-law. Everyone who told us that these people would shower their daughter-in-law (as precious as gold) with gold probably were fooled by their facade.

The family had gained the reputation of being a close-knit family. I believe that happened because of the strong influence Seethai had on her father. Since Chithi's mother was considered to be a tough and scheming woman, Seethai made sure that in the early days after her father married Chithi, the widowed mother did not move in with her to this house. It looked like Chithi was not only poor but was also very timid. Most of the young women from poor families had to marry older men who had children; they got married relatively later than other more wealthy girls, and also, they did not have much of a say in who they were married off to. However, this usually changed after the marriage since the older husband was invariably very accommodating to the young wife's foibles and let her run the show. The young woman would spend money freely and would buy herself nice clothes and jewellery that she could only dream of as a child. But in our house, Chithi could not exercise that much freedom. She was under the control of the stepdaughter Seethai. Chithi had very few jewels (even less than me), ditto for clothes too. She had to depend on her stepdaughter for everything. For many years Chithi seemed to live in fear of her stepdaughter. Only after her sons got married and she had her own daughters-in-law did she relax some and start protesting.

I recall an incident. Chithi's oldest son, Thanu, got married in Madras. As always, all preparations were controlled by Seethai. The second day after the wedding lunch, all of us gathered at noon at Thanu's house in Mylapore. Thanu, my father-in-law, Chithi, Thanu's new bride Kokila and her parents, and one other lady arrived around 5 p.m. By that time, Seethai had already started complaining that they were late.

She grumbled, "How could a father (referring to her own father) do this knowing Pappa (her younger sister) had to catch the evening train to return to Bombay?" She was pacing back and forth and her face was bright with anger. As soon as they stepped in, she became Kali, the angry goddess. She started yelling at her father, "Anna (my father-in-law was addressed as Anna, elder brother, by the children), you know that Pappa is leaving. How can you come so late? What was holding you up?" She continued her rant.

I don't remember all that she said that day. But I remember one thing clearly. At this point, Chithi couldn't take it anymore, and she interrupted Seethai saying, "What is your problem? Anyway we are here now and Pappa is yet to leave. You just want to find fault with everything." Chithi somehow developed the guts to say this.

Seethai retorted saying, "It is all fine for you to say whatever you want. You still have your mother."

Chithi in turn said, "You just can't stand it that I still have my mother."

On hearing this, Seethai started wailing and crying, hitting her chest and saying, "How could you say this to me? Do I behave that way? I have never discriminated against your children; I have treated them as equal to us. Oh, if I could just die!"

At this point Thanu immediately riposted, "Go ahead…Do it first!"

No other men were in the house at that time except for Thanu, my father-in-law and the bride's father. Perceiving that the situation was rapidly getting out of control, my father-in-law asked Chithi to apologize to Seethai. Thanu also joined in and pleaded with his mother to apologize. I guess that seeing both husband and son were on the same side, Chithi gave in and apologized to Seethai. As this high drama was unfolding, Pappa told Seethai several times to calm down. On my part, I felt that Seethai's tantrum was too much but I was too timid to say anything. Anyway, I was always at the receiving end of her spiteful remarks and was terrified of her. Every time she spoke to me she would invariably bring up the fact that I had the good fortune to have a mother who was still alive, while her mother was not.

One of the reasons for her irritation that day was the presence of Paatti (Chithi's mother). Paatti was sitting comfortably in a chair and shaking her legs, and Seethai made this snide comment, "Look at her. Sitting carefree in the chair shaking her legs!" Paatti heard this comment but chose to ignore it. After Chithi apologized, Thanu and my father-in-law consoled Seethai. Only after that did the virago cool off. Pappa left for Bombay with her husband, Srinivasan, and nine-year-old daughter, Rajalakshmi. Seethai, my father-in-law and Thanu went with them to the station to send them off.

Chithi felt deeply upset that this incident of wailing and beating the chest had happened at the time her daughter-in-law had entered the house for the first time.

She felt it was an inauspicious beginning for the newly-weds. The new in-laws including the bride (Kokila) were stunned and had little to say anyway. After returning to Vadiveeswaram, Chithi would recount the incident to neighbours and visitors who made courtesy calls and cry. She would repeat, "She behaved like it was a house of grief after bereavement. Oh! It is so inauspicious! It will bring bad luck to the newlyweds."

Hearing her lamenting, Paatti also told close friends, "It is my daughter who is to blame. All these years my daughter was so afraid of Seethai that she never did any-thing without her permission. Can someone throw such tantrums just because it got a little late? The main reason for Seethai's outburst was she did not like me being there and that is why she pointed out to my daughter that she had a mother. In fact, my daughter's reply to her saying, 'You can't stand me having a mother' was not in any way wrong." With all this stress, Chithi developed stomach cramps. I felt sorry for her, but could not help thinking how Chithi and Paatti used to gang up against me and join my sister-in-law Seethai when she used abusive lan-guage towards me.

Anyway, I also knew that after her son Thanu's wed-ding, Chithi would not be as timid as she used to be. She now had a daughter-in-law. Her children were growing up, and they would certainly stand by her. When I was relatively new to the family, Chithi would recount how her husband gave the entire collection of 100 sovereigns of gold belonging to his first wife to Seethai, his eldest daughter. He also gave his paternal aunt's jewels to his younger daughter Pappa and also bought more jewels for her. Her in-laws also demanded diamond studs as compensation for her dark complexion. He gifted her that too. The paternal aunt, Chithi mentioned, was my father-in-law's adoptive mother. His aunt had no children and had adopted my father-in-law. I came to know all this only through Chithi. Paatti would complain that many a second wife had been showered with jewellery but her daughter got nothing, and on top of that had to take care of the first wife's children like a servant. Even I felt that she had a point.

****

Chithi and Chellammal Get Diamond Ear Studs

After a few years of working for the *Ananda Vikatan* magazine, Thanu bought Chithi, his mother, a nose stud with three diamond stones, although I am not sure if it was a dual stud meant for both the nostrils. It was common to wear diamond nose studs on both nostrils. She would tell all visitors with pride that her son had bought her the jewellery with his earnings. After that she got diamond ear studs too.

When my father-in-law turned 60, Seethai decreed, "Anna is going to be 60. We should have a grand celebration. People from the entire street of Vadiveeswaram must be invited. (It was a street where only Brahmins resided.) We have to perform the *Rudra Ekadasi*[8] the day before." Father-in-law, as usual, agreed to everything that his daughter proposed. Not everyone who traditionally cele-

---

[8] Rudra Ekadasi is a mode of worship with a religious ritual with fire where *Rudram*, a Vedic chant in praise of Rudra, a form of Shiva, is chanted eleven times, to seek boons for human well-being, basically the boon of good health.

brated the sixtieth birthday performed the *Rudra Ekadasi* because it is entirely Vedic in nature. Preparations started in earnest months before the ceremony, but they did not buy clothing for family members, as was customary. Seethai gifted a rather ordinary silk sari to Chithi and a silk *veshti* to her father. Whether she bought them herself or my father-in-law paid for it was not clear. About four months before the function, Seethai brought home Azhagu Chettiar, a famous jeweller who specialized in making diamond jewels, from Madurai. She said she wanted Chithi to have diamond ear studs and had asked him to bring them. My father-in-law agreed and the studs were bought from the jeweller. I too got diamond ear studs. Now I will explain how the miracle of giving me a pair of studs came about from people who never gave me even a grain of gold.

It was about six months since my father's passing, and I was visiting Karamanai. Manni told me that she wanted her diamond ear studs and nose studs sold. She wanted the jewellery sold with Seethai's help. She needed the money and could not go out to sell the jewellery. She felt that Seethai would have the contacts. She gave me the ear studs and told me that I could wear them till the sale was done. I was not keen on wearing the studs but I brought the diamond studs with me when I returned to Vadiveeswaram. I showed the studs to Chithi and Paatti and explained the matter. They said, "You should buy them for yourself. The pair will look good on you. The diamonds are really sparkling." When Seethai came home I told her what Manni had told me, and she told me to keep the studs at home and that she would ask around.

She came after two days and took the studs with her. Then she returned them saying that she had asked a few people and that they were quoting a very low price for the pair of studs.

At that point, Paatti and Chithi said, "Why don't we buy this for Chellammal? Her mother seems to have some financial hardship and needs the money, and will probably be willing to accept a lower amount. After all, the jewellery would then go to her daughter. And anyway, we have not given her any jewellery for the *Kanyadanam* ceremony during the wedding. This would make up for that." Seethai half-heartedly agreed and said she would ask my father-in-law. I was 25 years old then. I must admit I was somewhat surprised to see Chithi and Paatti intercede on my behalf. Manni's ear studs alone were some thousand rupees worth. They were bought many years ago but Manni had worn them not more than a year or so. They finally bought both the ear studs and the nose studs for 750 rupees. Manni was happy that the jewellery had stayed within the family and had come to me. I was also thrilled.

I wore the studs for the first time when I visited our neighbour and my dear friend Muthu Mami. Both mother and daughters were all praise and commented on the lustre of the studs, and I told them, "I don't know how they look on me but when my Manni used to wear the studs, they would indeed glow and meld with her round face and flawless complexion."

My friends then said, "You look just as good."

Father-in-law's sixtieth birthday was celebrated with great pomp and ceremony. Vaidyanathan was also married by then. His wife, Valli, was six or seven months pregnant. After a full term, the child died in the womb. The delivery took place at her parental home in Valliyur. Later, her first daughter and son were born in Vadiveeswaram. All the women who had come for the celebration noticed and praised the diamond studs and the nose studs that I was wearing. "So Seethai ultimately gave you the bridal gift that she had promised," they remarked. I wore a light orange-coloured six-yard sari, the diamonds and nose studs and all my other jewellery and had a whole bunch of fragrant jasmine flowers on my hair; they had bought the best flowers available in Thovalai for the ceremony. Looking at myself with my long thick hair decorated with flowers in the mirror, I could not help admiring myself and thinking how beautiful I was!

****

My Friend Padmavathi

As I have said before, Seethai disliked Muthu Mami and tried to prevent me from visiting their house. She would say that Muthu Mami was a cheat and would destroy a good family and also that people considered her characterless. But for me, visiting their house was one of the few sources of happiness that I experienced. I made it a point to visit their house at least once a day. Muthu Mami stayed with her third daughter for a few years. Her second daughter Gnanam lived a little farther away within Vadiveeswaram with her husband. She was married to her first cousin, a common custom. Gnanam, like her mother, was tall, buxom and good looking. She was seven years younger than me, but we were close friends. The older daughter Sundari's husband was my husband's friend. He was in the military and so Sundari stayed with her mother. The youngest daughter Saroja's husband worked in Canara Bank, and he stayed with the same bank in Nagercoil till he retired. Even when Mami and her daughters moved into independent houses they continued to live in the same town. Despite my sister-in-law speaking ill of them, I continued to maintain my friendship with the family.

Another close friend was Padmavathi. She was known as Pavu. I would like to write about her in detail. When I returned to this living hell that is my marital home in Vadiveeswaram, five months after the birth of my first daughter Shobha, Pavu was living across our house in a tenement called Mangala. It was a slum colony that had been named Mangala. The place did not even have the basic amenities. Some of those homes still exist to this day, almost 60 years later. But now most of the houses have electricity, a gas stove, running water and flushing toilets. All of them have extended their houses at the back, encroaching into the space belonging to the municipality. Even with the additions and improvements they still have to live with the stench of the open sewer running behind their homes. It is only recently that they have been closing these sewer drains in many places around the town. Hopefully, that will be done here too.

Pavu had fought with her father and had moved into one of those homes with her mother, younger sister and brother. Her mother was the second wife. The first wife had six or seven children. Apparently, Pavu's father had owned a lot of property and somehow lost it over the years, and in any case, he did not seem to have a steady job. She was learning vocal music from this person called Raman who was then living in the next village known as Nagercoil Gramam. Raman wrote music and scripts for plays, and due to the economic situation in her house, Pavu acted in some of those plays whenever there was an opportunity. Raman was also training her in Puranic story narration interspersed with songs known as *Kathakalak-shebam*. Raman was related to my husband Chidambaram from his mother's side; one could say he was a maternal uncle. He also had a house in our village Vadiveeswaram. His siblings lived in that house while Raman stayed in his wife's place in Nagercoil Gramam.

Raman's wife had some mental problems. It was said that her problems were caused by Pavu. Raman later moved into his Vadiveeswaram house with Pavu. Pavu's mother and siblings stayed in the Mangala tenement house, while Pavu had meals at her mother's place but otherwise spent most of the time with Raman at his place. Besides mentoring and teaching Pavu to give *Kathakalakshabam* performances, Raman also acted as her agent in negotiating the right price for the concerts. He also accompanied her when she went to give concerts. All in all, he was in complete charge of her life. He also handled all the money that was received for her performances. If she needed money for her personal expenses she would take it from him. She had great respect and affection for him.

Pavu became a popular performer only after moving to Vadiveeswaram. She was quite good looking and only 16 when she first moved into the tenement across our house. She was two years younger than me. Just like me, she looked good in almost any kind of sari, and all jewellery suited her. Whenever she had some spare time she would visit me, and sometimes my father-in-law would talk to her. Interestingly enough, over a period of time, he would even share the details of his salary and his property with her. Pavu was very fond of my first child, Shobha. So was Mama (which is what I called Raman). Pavu would take my daughter to her house often, and both of them would shower affection on my baby girl. They would buy her biscuits, toys and other eatables.

Their immense affection for my child was revealed in one incident. My girl was four years old then. One day she fell from our doorstep and broke her arm. In those days, practitioners of the indigenous medicine system, who were known as Asans or masters who had specialized in fixing broken bones, treated fractures. One such traditional bone setter treated my daughter and put a bandage on her arm. My husband usually had no faith in our traditional indigenous medical practices, but for some reason he allowed this treatment for our daughter. I did not have much of a say in the matter. While she was recuperating, Raman Mama would carry her to the nearby Pioneer movie theatre to entertain her. In those days, they would start playing the movie songs an hour before the actual start of the movie. Raman always said that my daughter enjoyed the music.

I am absolutely certain that Shobha's interest and aptitude for music came from me. I used to memorize the lyrics and music of all the movie songs, but I did not dare sing them in our house. Even humming a tune was not tolerated by my father-in-law. I remember that once I was humming my favourite tune from, I think, the movie *Sakuntala*, when Seethai came up to me and curtly said, "Anna is not well. You are singing without any consideration for his health; he doesn't like it." From the time I arrived at my in-laws' place, all I can remember about my father-in-law was his constant obsession with his bodily functions and his health. He would keep complaining about minor ailments like constipation and insomnia and at times make them seem like some major disease. During those times he would become disinterested in anything else. He would stop going to court. A person would come to give him herbal decoctions and massage his hair with medicinal oil. Finally, he would become okay with one medicine or the other. This would happen now and then. As time went by, his mental illness and obsessions increased. All through the night, he would keep calling out to his son (my husband) who would be sleeping upstairs in our bedroom. He used to get angry at the slightest noise and would throw a tantrum if someone (especially me) so much as breathed heavily. If he was unwell and I went out with my friends to watch a movie, he would be very bitter and resentful when I returned and make it obvious by grumbling, "A person in the house is dying and nobody cares."

Since Chithi had to open the house door to let me in, she and her mother would also complain. Paatti would say, "Why do you have to be like a servant to her and get up to open the door? It gets to be 10 in the night by the time she comes. And we are forced to keep food out for her and cannot wrap up the kitchen work."

When my children were five or six years old, I would ask my husband to put them to bed while I was gone. At that age, the children did not need much supervision, but the moment I said I was going to see a movie, Paatti would make it a point to ask, "Who will serve the children their food?" As if giving the children their food was an insurmountable task!

This family had a reputation in the village, quite justified, for treating the stepchildren well. My two older sisters-in-law were as affectionate towards the three sons of their stepmother as they were towards their own biological siblings. Whatever was done was done without any discrimination. They also treated the wives of those stepbrothers well. But I was the only daughter-in-law who had to live in the joint family, and I was mistreated. I did not have anyone to champion my cause. Not that I needed anyone. I could have opposed any kind of injustice myself. But then I was timid and lacked courage. I did not fear Chithi as much as I feared my sister-in-law, but there was Chithi's mother standing by her like a rock. My friend Pavu would often say, "To add insult to injury, you have this Paatti also to deal with."

As Pavu's income increased she bought silk saris and jewellery. I remember she bought special kind of silk sari known as "tissue" sari,[9] entirely woven with gold threads. The cost of the sari must have been 250 or 300 rupees, rather expensive in those days. She tried to talk me into getting a similar sari. I had just then started wearing six-yard saris.

I told her, "You know my situation and yet you say this. I cannot even spend five rupees at my own whim and fancy."

She countered saying, "You should be smart enough to argue with your husband and make him buy you one. I know you keep saying your husband is not earning much but your father-in-law is wealthy. Why can't your husband ask him for some money?" And she went on this way.

I replied, "That will never happen but I am tempted. I have some money left over from gifts given to my children

---

[9] The term "tissue" came from the glass tissue fabric used in these saris.

by friends and relatives. Actually, I could buy the sari with that money, but then I can't wear it in this house. Everyone (including Paatti) would question me about it. Not only that, my sister-in-law would have no qualms blaming Muthu Mami for being a bad influence on me."

Pavu would then remark, "What is the point of being so wealthy when you are not fortunate enough to enjoy it?"

Pavu was a very nice person. There was a 25-year difference in age between her and Raman Mama. He looked very thin but Pavu liked him a lot, and they had an intimate relationship. Pavu had mentioned that in her conversations with me. There was so much age difference and he was not all that good looking either. I know why Pavu liked Raman. Pavu knew him from a very young age. He wrote songs and scripts for plays. He taught her music and took her to many *Kathakalakshebam* performances. Raman also drew pictures and did beautiful paintings. During Navaratri festival he would have a beautiful *Golu*, arrangement of dolls, at his house and his artistry was showcased in that exhibit. As a matter of fact, he was popularly known as "Artist" Raman. Despite all his talents, he did not make any special efforts to utilize them. So he did not achieve much recognition, and his talents remained hidden for all purposes. I have heard that the famous Tamil film Music Director K.V. Mahadevan initially learned music from Raman, and I know that Mahadevan visited their house once when Pavu was not getting many opportunities to perform. This was, I believe, when Mahadevan was also losing his popularity in the movie industry. When Mahadevan visited, a crowd gathered around their house. I was watching all this from my doorstep, and Pavu filled me in on the details of the visit. Apparently, he paid his respects to Raman in the traditional manner by falling at his feet. However, Raman pointed out that Mahadevan had been ignoring him. At this juncture, Mahadevan apologized and said he would make amends, and left. They never heard from him after that. Raman Mama was a proud man and that is probably why he could not get ahead in his professional career.

When Pavu's performances had gained notice, once when Pavu and Raman Mama were visiting Thirumangalam town for a performance, they ate at a local restaurant. The young man who served their table was handsome, soft-spoken, and they liked him very much. Pavu immediately felt he would be a good match for her younger sister, so she promptly asked him if he was married and when he said he was not, told him, "I have a sister who is good looking and soft natured. Will you marry her?"

The young man immediately replied, "Come to our house and speak with my mother and elder brother." He took permission from his boss at the restaurant and immediately the three of them left for Venkateeswaran's (that was the young man's name) house. The wedding talks were finalized then and there, and Pavu and Raman Mama returned home. Venkateeswaran was apparently so impressed by Pavu's looks and status that he agreed to the wedding without setting eyes on Pavu's sister.

Another important event happened soon. I am not sure if it was in Madurai or Thirumangalam. I think Madurai station comes after Thirumangalam. Pavu performed in both places, so I don't remember. Pavu and Raman themselves got married in a temple between Madurai and Thirumangalam, the town where they had gone to perform. Pavu was then 25 and Raman was 50. Pavu's sister Kutti's wedding took place after theirs, in Thirumangalam at Venkateeswaran's house. I went to Pavu's sister's wedding with my son Ambi. I saw Madurai for the first time then. I did not have much money but bought some bangles and vermillion powder used for the *pottu*. My son was only four years old then, and I don't think I bought anything for him. We saw all the important spots in Madurai—the Meenakshi Temple, Thirumalai Nayakan Hall, the pavilion with a thousand pillars, the Temple Tank, etc. We were escorted by a local couple who took us (a party of five) to their house. It was a big house shared by four or five families. Even in those days Madurai was very congested. I have visited Madurai four times since then. The temple has beautiful sculptures. It is a huge temple and you can get lost and forget which gate you entered by. There are many huge temples in Tamil Nadu but they are mostly dedicated to male gods, but only in Madurai do they have this humongous ancient temple for goddess Meenakshi.

Once I returned home, all the joy of visiting Madurai vanished in a few seconds. No one said this to me directly but their faces expressed disapproval. Paatti told our neighbour in my presence, "My daughter is not able to go anywhere. And there is her illness that is a constant bother. So no one takes her out anywhere. Having married this old man she is fated only to slog for him and his first wife's children. The second wives I know rule their husbands so."

The neighbour Valli heard her out and said, "You are so right. There can be no one like your daughter. Go and have your food. It is getting late," and then got up and left. Most of these conversations happened on the patio from 11 a.m. to 5 p.m. At least three or four women between the ages of Chithi and Paatti would gather to gossip, and they would talk and complain about the happenings in various houses on the street. They never seemed to realize their own shortcomings.

Pavu and Raman threw a party for their close friends and family to indicate they were married, when they returned home after Kutti's wedding. Within a few months of Kutti's wedding, she returned home. Venkateeswaran dropped Kutti off saying that she is having a hard time dealing with the in-laws. He visited often and would send money every month. Within a year after the wedding, he had established his own restaurant. Later he moved the restaurant from Thirumangalam to a place called Kottampatti. That was also near Madurai, I think. All buses going to Chennai and Trichy would stop at Venkateeswaran's restaurant for lunch. He had a good reputation and the restaurant did roaring business, so he would send a lot of money to Pavu.[10] He would also send fruits, vegetables and provisions to Pavu in buses coming to Nagercoil from Kottampatti. All the drivers and conductors were his friends. Venkateeswaran was friendly with everyone and looked calm and unruffled. Within a year of his marriage to Kutti she gave birth to a girl, who was brought up with great love and affection. When the girl, Vijaya, was four

---

[10] Pavu would handle the purse strings in the family.

years old, Venkateeswaran disappeared. He was gone for four years and returned when she was eight. I don't remember where and why he was gone. After his return, he resumed sending money to the family and he continued to own the restaurant in Kotampatti. Since Pavu made good money through her concerts she did not skimp on spending for Vijaya.

When Vijaya was seven or eight years old, Pavu gave birth to a baby girl, Srimathi. Three years later she had a son. There was gossip by women that Raman did not father her two children. One of the women who maligned Pavu and her children in this fashion was my husband's brother's wife, Valli. I had a different take. Everyone says that children are the gift of god. Why can't they accept these children also similarly?

Pavu was young, attractive and was working and making good money. She was married to this elderly man and in many ways was under his control. She gave all her income to him and would spend for herself only with his permission. Society allows a man to be intimate and have relationships with multiple women. Many a man with means would have a second woman in his life and blatantly set up a second household with her. That in no way seemed to affect his standing in society. On the other hand, if a woman had an extramarital affair, the neighbouring women, both young and old, would call her a prostitute. They also had disparaging names for widows and infertile women, labelling them "barren" and "wasted", even though more than half the cases of infertility were due to issues with the man. Such language is not just used by the women in villages. Even the so-called sophisticated women in the cities speak this way. I think I have written about it elsewhere in this journal.

Most married women, be it the first wife or the second wife, did not exactly overflow with love for their husbands. Fear of society, blind beliefs and having nowhere to go made many women conform and suppress their own needs and go on with their lives in a servile manner. As far as Pavu was concerned, she respected her husband a lot. She loved him. She would never do anything without his approval. She was proud of him and spoke highly of him. "I have come up in life because of him. He is so talented, can write scripts, songs, set tunes, draw, and paint, but he is not lucky enough to get a break," she would lament. I would say that Raman did not really try enough to promote his talent, and Pavu would agree with me.

When Pavu's career took a downturn it was Venkateeswaran who continued to help her family. After Kutti's daughter Vijaya got a bachelor's degree in commerce, she immediately got a job in Vijaya Bank. Although she was short, Vijaya was fair and good-looking. Her wedding was conducted in a grand manner by Venkateeswaran. The wedding tent was very aesthetically done. In those days many artisans could put up a beautiful tent depending on the budget. For the engagement ceremony in Madurai, Pavu took me with her in a taxi. Vijaya's husband's family was from Madurai. Many young men who attended the wedding apparently were drawn to Pavu's teenage daughter, Srimathi. The daughter was tall, dark-complexioned and very pretty. She had a beautiful smile and when she smiled her teeth looked like perfect pearls. The gossip mill said that she was happily chatting with all those boys. I did not think there was anything wrong about a young girl being attracted and trying to converse with boys of her age. In fact, the boys may have been even more attracted to her than she was to them.

When I pointed that out, it did not go well with the two women who were gossiping. They said, "These are all bad times. Like mother, like daughter. You are, after all, Pavu's friend. Now, don't go and report to her about our conversation here." I thought to myself how deceitful these people are. When they see Pavu they change their tone and praise her about her talent and her concerts, saying she makes them feel as though goddess Saraswati herself was performing. Many of the Puranic stories have themes that put down women. Many don't even consider these as mere stories. They feel that listening to the stories reveals life's truths to them. But Pavu was thrilled to hear their praises. She was usually invited to all functions in the neighbourhood, and at one time was the reigning queen of the Harikatha concert scene in Nagercoil.

Later in life, as Pavu's income dwindled, she did not have economic difficulties because Vijaya, who had settled in the US, periodically sent some 50 or 100 dollars. Pavu's own daughter, Srimathi, also completed college and started to work in the Vijaya Bank, same as Vijaya. At some point, Pavu did not have any more of the *Kathakalakshebams*. She then started doing South Indian classical music concerts. Her knowledge and technique were good but her performance lacked soul. Also, she would go off-tune at times, maybe because she had not trained under the tutelage of an established guru.

Pavu's son, Ganesan, was not of much help to her. With great financial hardship, she put him through college, but he did not make much use of it. He has a wonderful wife. She is the breadwinner for the family and seems to have great respect for her husband. Theirs was a marriage of their choice. They have two children who are good at studies. The elder son is doing his engineering, and I am not sure about where the daughter is studying. But I know she is going to a good school. I can keep on talking about Pavu but am not physically fit enough to do that. I have a lot more to write about. I have to write it even if it is a truncated version.

Raman Mama died when he was 88. Besides the dollars that Vijaya sent, Pavu earned some money by teaching music to children from well-to-do families of doctors, businessmen and lawyers on the other side of town. She would go around 10 a.m. and come back by 4 p.m. I believe she made about 1,000 rupees a month. After all, she was not a famous singer. So they would not pay her much. But give her biscuits, coffee, tiffin, etc. Also, they treated her with respect and affection.

Pavu ultimately fell sick. She was bedridden for a month. Even at that time, she managed to take care of her toilet needs herself without anyone's help. She was diagnosed with cancer. She started having pain in her neck and it slowly became intolerable. She had a scan and they found out it was cancer. She was admitted for treatment in Neyyoor hospital about 16 km away. When they got to know about her illness, her younger sister's son Ravi (almost 15 years younger than Vijaya) who was working in Chennai and her daughter Srimathi who was in Goa came to see her. Ravi was a very good-natured young man and treated Pavu with affection. He also helped Pavu with some money. While all this was happening, I was away at my brother's place in Thiruvananthapuram. When I returned home with my brother Ganapathi, I was shocked to find out that Pavu had cancer. Ganapathi knew her well and he visited her in the hospital. She told him that her neck pain was much improved and that she expected to be well after the completion of the ongoing radiation treatments. Ganapathi said she did not seem to understand the gravity of the situation and hopefully, everything would turn out well and she would return home. When I went to visit her, she told me that her pain was under control but that the radiation treatment was being interrupted as the machine needed to be repaired. Hearing this, Valli (my husband's brother's wife) who had accompanied me remarked, "What kind of a hospital is this? How come they don't have a second machine? How can they take so much time to repair such an important machine? How come they do not have a spare?" I must admit I also felt the same way.

Pavu looked very calm and composed. Her sister Kutti (Vijaya's mother) arrived to help her. Her daughter Srimathi called me from Goa and asked me to report on how her mother was doing. She said she and her husband could take Pavu with them to Goa if needed. By then it was four days since I had last visited Pavu in the hospital, where she seemed to be okay. I told Srimathi I would send our driver Chettiar to check on Pavu. I explained everything to the driver and asked him to go and see if Pavu was okay. He went and met Pavu and told her what her daughter had said over the phone. He returned saying Pavu had told him she was feeling better and expected to be discharged soon. She did not want Srimathi to come. I relayed that to Srimathi over the phone. But within a week Pavu died of a severe heart attack. It happened at 3 a.m. and only her younger sister was at her bedside. Soon, her daughter Srimathi, son-in-law Kannan and Kutti's son Ravi arrived for her last journey. Many attended her last rites but I had just had an eye operation and I could not go. (For one eye the operation was done in Aravind Hospital in Tirunelveli. After the operation when I opened that eye I could only see bright light. It took a while to heal. The second eye was operated in Madras and that did not trouble me much.) My brother Ganapathi, who had come to help me during the operation, did attend the cremation. I was deeply affected by Pavu's loss. For a long time, I thought about various incidents and sank into deep grief. It has been eight years since I have lost my dearest friend who was younger than me. I console myself saying she did not have to be bedridden for long and this was the best way for her to go. As far as possible, I have tried to keep this note on Padmavathi short. I find it difficult to write these days. But I do enjoy writing although it is becoming more and more difficult. But I feel that I have to somehow finish what I have begun. Now I will come back to matters concerning me.

****

Bhagavathi from Palla Street

Bhagavathi lived on the next street, Palla Street, where my sister-in-law Seethai also lived. She was a close friend of Seethai, although she was almost 20 years younger. Both of them went everywhere together and like good friends, shared everything with each other. All those who lived on that street and who were formerly quite deferential to Seethai slowly moved under the wing of Bhagavathi. The women of Palla Street, led by Bhagavathi, got together and formed a Ladies Club called Ambal Mandali, meaning the Team of the Goddess.[11] Some women from the neighbouring streets like Dhalavai Street and Periya Street also joined them. During the festival of Navaratri they would go to the local temple of the goddess Azhagamman after 10 p.m. and offer special prayers and recite chants. They would also sing, although none of them could really hold a tune in my opinion.

I have heard that many non-Brahmin women joined the club and donated saris, skirt pieces and blouse pieces

---

[11] The reason for calling it so may be because there is a famous temple for the goddess Mutharamman in Vadiveeswaram and also another temple for the goddess Azahagamman.

to Bhagavathi telling her to distribute them to any poor or needy women of her choice. Bhagavathi was not caste conscious. During various religious festivals, the members would offer money for offering prayers to the goddess. However, the members of the group would get together to prepare the various snacks and puddings to be given as offerings to the goddess. Bhagavathi stayed away from the stove even at her home, where she always had a cook. She liked to order people around. She also liked shopping. It did not exactly mean buying everything that was needed. Seethai and she would make several trips to the stores. But the puddings and snacks made for the offerings were not all that tasty. They tasted like what Seethai herself would make at home. The necessary quantity of jaggery, ghee, cashew nuts and cardamom would not be added. I often wondered if they saved on these because they knew that the god was not going to taste it at all in any case. I never joined in any of the religious celebrations of the club but during important festivals like Navaratri and Karthikai, I would go to the temple. Once or twice around midday out of curiosity, I went to see what these women were up to. Once when I went I saw these young women singing, with Bhagavathi just pacing up and down, not singing or doing much. Even the traditional distribution of the *prasadam* was done by the other women.

We may not have made many discoveries compared to other countries but when it comes to consuming food it seems like no other country can beat us Indians. All year round there are religious festivals big and small. Among the Hindus, the non-Brahmins also have many rituals and ceremonies like naming the newborn, ear-piercing of the child and melting the gold for the *thali*. There is also the age-old custom celebrated almost like another marriage in the odd months after the marriage, of removing the *thali* and adding different shaped small symbolic gold decorations to it and getting it blessed by elders and wearing it again. The most important ritual is when the girl attains menarche; however poor a person is, it would be celebrated grandly. However, though money had to be spent by the immediate family, one could also expect reasonable monetary gifts from the relatives. The Brahmins also celebrate this occasion not in such a grand manner but it is celebrated to symbolize a girl turning into a woman. I have written in detail about this celebration earlier in this journal. Bhagavathi would attend all the functions. As I said before, she did not care about caste differences.

Bhagavathi seemed so god-fearing in every way, but when it came to caring about her husband Sundaram, she seemed indifferent. Her husband was unable to hold a steady job. At a later stage, he completely quit working and trying to get a job. Maybe because of that, Bhagavathi had no love or respect for him. She raised her two sons and a daughter with the help of her parents. Her daughter later settled in America. Her children used to send her money. When Sundaram fell and broke his leg, Bhagavathi went to check on him just once but never attended to him, and he was fully taken care of by a servant. They lived in the house that belonged to Bhagavathi's parents. Sundaram lived upstairs. They had a cook who would serve him food, coffee, etc. Or he would come down and have his food. The upstairs portion also had all the conveniences. Bhagavathi and her husband rarely spoke to each other. Bhagavathi was on medication for a variety of problems, including high blood pressure and heart disease. Though she hardly did any work at home she sprang into action if there was a medical emergency in a neighbour's house. She would immediately go there and stay with the patient and the family till they were transported safely to the hospital. She even provided first aid. So, her indifferent attitude towards her husband at the time of his illness (he broke his leg twice, in fact) surprised me. Both Bhagavathi and her husband are no more. Bhagavathi was bedridden for two years before she passed away. Her husband, Sundaram, has now been gone for five years. He never had it good. He was a good man but I do not think he had an easy end to his life, which leads me to believe that whatever happens to people does not have anything to do with their character as such.

Bhagavathi had an enduring interest and passion for making handicrafts with wool, beads, etc. She made many bags and they were beautiful. I am not sure if they were all made to sell, but she did make vermillion powder used by women to keep *pottu* on their forehead in her house for sale. She would also bring in synthetic silk saris (popular then) from out of town and sell them. She was really talented in many ways. I was not planning to write so much about Bhagavathi but then decided I had to say something since she was indeed a prominent figure in Vadiveeswaram. I used to attend all functions at her house, and she also would come for all the events at our house. I don't remember if she attended the sacred thread ceremony of my son Ambi (Neelakantan). It is possible she came for the party and left soon after that because for her Seethai was the important person in our family.

****

An Open Conversation
with Chidambaram

Eventually my husband Chidambaram (that is how everyone called him) started earning an income (as a lawyer), when he turned thirty-five. It was my father-in-law who was responsible for that. Prior to that he tried to make money in the stock market. Three men headed by my husband started a small firm. My husband had borrowed 15,000 rupees from my father-in-law for the initial expenses. By that time my father-in-law's law practice was declining and he was looking for other ways to make money. I don't know anything about stocks, shares, etc. All I know is that very soon the enterprise failed and there was a loss. By then my father-in-law was constantly complaining about his health problems—constipation, insomnia and so on. And he would turn into a real patient. And then there would be various treatments. Not only did he suffer but he made others suffer too.

When the share market enterprise collapsed, he was shattered. He told my husband, "You caused this loss. Do you realize how hard it is to earn 15,000 rupees?" I felt that he was right in asking this question. From that time onwards my father-in-law stopped going to court. Even when he did, it was half-hearted, so my husband took over. Initially, the clients were hesitant to work with my husband, but as time went by they became more confident and his caseload increased.

I remember once that the authorities banned a particular movie screening in Nagercoil. The theatre owners came to Chidambaram and told him, "You should somehow initiate legal action to lift the ban. We have to screen the film today. We will run into big loss otherwise." I do not know what he did but that film was screened the same day in the theatre. The theatre owners came and garlanded him. That sealed his reputation! This was about a year after he started making an income.

Meanwhile, my father-in-law continued his rants convinced that he was seriously ill. "I won't live long. I am constipated. I have insomnia. You don't care for me. I have lost a big amount. I have no income to talk of," and so on.

My husband's usual reply was, "I do buy you all the medications. I will earn and pay you back all the money and more. But if you are depressed and keep crying, that will affect me. Also, being constipated and lack of sleep are not serious health issues. You must calm down. Only if you are happy can I do my job without worries." When my father-in-law could not sleep, he would keep calling out to his son.

As my husband's income increased, he took over all the expenses in the house. The medicines alone would cost about 200 rupees a month. We got 2,000 rupees a year by selling rice from our paddy fields. Father-in-law wanted my husband to take that money, but instead, my husband offered to put it in an account for him. Once, my father-in-law said to my husband, "I hear you are getting famous. Everyone talks highly about your skills in court. That makes me very happy. In some ways, it seems like it was a good thing that I got sick. You also seem to be very responsible now."

However, nothing changed for me. I was hoping to have more money to spend, but even if I just bought a piece of cloth to get a blouse stitched, my father-in-law would throw a fit, as though I was frittering all my husband's wealth. He would not allow the tailor to come to the house, and I could not even have the goldsmith work in the house on reworking my old gold. I could not buy new clothes. If I bought a simple new sari and clothes for my children for Deepavali festival, he would use hurtful words to criticize, and just a few rupees worth of firecrackers for the festive season would bring forth some more harsh words for me.

My second son Kumar was born about four years after my husband started earning an income. Since I did not have the means to get the fancy Lactogen infant formula and nourishing Glaxo biscuits for my older children, I decided to have a child just to feed those to my new baby. I did not care if it was a boy or girl, I just wanted another child. That child was Kumar. Since I myself was from a poor family, I considered these new-fangled nutrition products a luxury and used them with utmost care and frugality, but even then, my father-in-law would yell as though I was draining all our income. As time went by my father-in-law spent most of the time inside the house and constantly used hurtful and spiteful language.

Going back to the Deepavali story, it was a long time—21 years—after coming to this house that I finally bought a silk sari for myself for Deepavali and that too after a lot of persuasion by Pavu. She said someone in the next street had brought saris from Tirunelveli.

"Those people live in Periya Theru. It is a mango-colour sari with a broad brocade border costing about 150 rupees. It is beautiful. Let me get two saris for both of us," she said.

I told her I did not want a sari and that if I wore the sari it will create a big ruckus in the house. Pavu told me even people who were not so well off had bought the saris and that I should not be so timid when my husband was earning well. She said I will kill myself this way and left saying she was going to pick up the sari anyway, whether I wanted it or not.

That night I told my husband about it. I said I could not joyfully wear a new sari since inevitably, his father would object.

"Even though you have a good income I can't buy myself anything. So long as I am here my situation will not change," I told him.

My husband remarked that he cannot tell his father anything; all he could do was give me the money and that I should just do what I wanted and not bother about comments from others.

(I stopped writing here and began to think. As people grow old, they start believing in things they never did before. I mean, like going to temples, performing *pooja* and rituals, etc. In short, they get drawn to whatever has been prescribed by the caste elders as being meritorious. As far as I am concerned, I can say that I have lost even the few beliefs that I had earlier. I ponder now over all that has been said. Everything seems like a lie. They say it is all god's will. I also tell that to myself for writing this. The blind beliefs related to god can never be true devotion. The realized sages have always said that god has endowed human beings with wisdom and that they must use their wisdom to function. I don't know how others look at this but it appeals to me. Sometimes I am stricken by the thought that I have wasted my energy and time in writing this. Now back to my story.)

Incidents that regularly happened in my life kept reminding me that life had placed me in an unenviable position where I had to bear the brunt of relationships that existed within the joint family. One day, all of a sudden, Chidambaram told my father-in-law that he would like to perform the *Poonul*, for Ambi, my elder son. My father-in-law said he could not afford to spend the money, and my husband replied, "No worries, I will take care of all the expenses."

I told my husband, "I thought you didn't care for these rituals."

He replied, "That is true, but I am doing well now, and have always wanted to have some kind of celebration in the family. This will be a good occasion."

I merely said, "Is that so?" and left it at that.

Preparations for the *Poonul* began. I went to Mudukku in Thiruvananthapuram to invite people to the function. (My sister-in-law Seethai was living in Thiruvananthapuram at that time.) I had taken my child Kumar along. Of course, I went to visit my people in Karamanai, which was on the way.

I told Manni about the ceremony. She said, "I have rarely visited your house. Even on those few occasions, your sister-in-law would not speak to me. I won't be able to actively participate, in any case. (Widows were not supposed to be prominently present during auspicious ceremonies and celebrations.) Your sister-in-law will do the needful."

I told her, "It has been eight years since Anna passed away. You should not stay indoors cooped up like this. You must come."

She said, "You really don't call the shots in your house and it is your sister-in-law who rules and decides. I have not visited you even when I was not a widow. How can I come now?"

I feel like repeating this again and again. I don't know how many times I have said this in my life story. No other religion has been as cruel to widows as the Hindu religion. Even now in movies and TV serials, the widows appear in white saris. I looked at her face (which was devoid of all jewellery, as was required for widows) and I instantly felt extreme anger towards this society. For the past eight years, she has not worn jewellery. It was not something new to me. Progressive people like me do get annoyed when we are confronted with the practice of widows not being able to attend auspicious occasions. Manni did not believe in blindly accepting such dictums, yet she conformed to the expectations of the society. I had to comfort myself in the thought that there has been some progress in terms of liberating widows. In those days, on the tenth day of the husband's passing, society and customs required that the widow completely shave her hair and stay tonsured for the rest of her life. Also, from that point onwards, she was supposed to only wear a white sari covering her body and head, irrespective of her age. The person who would initiate her into this kind of existence would be another young or old widow.

The non-Brahmins did not tonsure the widow but they too followed all other customs of degrading the widow in terms of appearance and functioning in the society. They had many other rituals too. Even if a woman is a young widow, all these rituals are observed. All the relatives would come and cover her with a white sari. In Brahmin households, the widow would be given a white sari from her parental home. Nowadays they also buy a few coloured saris. I saw the ritual detailed in a recent TV serial. Most of the serials have stories revolving around non-Brahmin families. Despite caste differences, the customs would be similar.

In the TV drama I mentioned, there was this middle-aged widow, dressed in a beautiful sari wearing jewellery, glass bangles, the traditional *kunkumam pottu* on her forehead and her hair decked with flowers. Then some other widows surrounded her and ceremoniously took away her jewellery, broke the bangles, took off the flowers, rubbed off the *pottu* from her forehead and had her wear a white sari. So ended that day's episode, which deeply saddened me. However, in the next day's episode, the newly widowed woman appeared dressed in her usual clothes! It seemed like the show's producers

had to go through the motions of showing the traditional widowhood ceremony at least once to conform to the
expectations of the society and the viewers, especially the
women among them. These traditions are so deeply ingrained that it is hard to shake them off all at once. I have
not seen such elaborate rituals involving the entire village
among the Brahmins.

I am not sure if other women feel as distressed as I
do on seeing such practices that I have mentioned above.
Older women seem to be even less bothered. Women have
progressed a lot but it has happened only in the urban
areas. But even modern households observe the practice
of excluding widows and preventing them from fully participating in auspicious occasions and ceremonies. At least
nowadays the widows are seated with everyone else, unlike in those days where they had to remain out of sight.
However, at many weddings today, even when the widows are sitting with other married women, when it comes
to offering flowers and *kumkumam*[12] to greet the women
guests, they are bypassed and ignored. It was in this context that Manni commented on her not being welcome to
the *Poonul* ceremony of my son. Although I was getting
used to seeing Manni not wearing any jewellery, inter-
mittently I would be filled with sadness. Seeing Manni's
absolutely flawless face I could only imagine how beautiful it would be to see her once again with the dark red dot
on her forehead, the dazzling diamond ear studs and the
solitaire nose ring that she used to wear. She still looked
good even when she wore drab clothes. You could not tell

---

[12] The conservative and orthodox traditions of the past forbade wom-
en from wearing the *kunkumam pottu*.

she was 56. She was slim and did not have any grey hair. Even my hair started turning grey only after I turned 70.

After our discussion, she told me, "Get going. Go to your sister-in-law's place. I will have your brother Natarajan go with you. He will help you carry Kumar (my baby son)."

I told her, "I can't wait till he comes. I will manage," and I took a shortcut. I had to go up an incline and it was hard carrying Kumar on my hip. Thiruvananthapuram roads were not even.

At one point I passed a number of young men who were chatting. As I passed they said "not bad". I looked back to see who they were referring to but did not see anyone else, and so I concluded that the comment was intended for me.

Then I heard this other voice from behind me saying, "Lady, wait." An older gentleman approached me.

He said, "You are the daughter of Kesava Iyer, aren't you? I knew him well. I heard what these guys were saying. It is very common in this place to make such comments if a woman looks good. They don't even stop if the woman is a respectable married woman with a child. I will escort you."

I replied, "I am almost there. I will manage. Thank you very much."

He said, "No problem. Should I not do at least this much for the daughter of Kesava Iyer whom I knew? I also have a good-looking daughter like you, and I can walk with you till you reach your place."

I told him, "No need. Actually the house is just next to where I am now standing."

He left saying, "Don't bother about what those guys said."

I thought to myself: Why is he making this such a serious issue? The young guys didn't say anything objectionable. In fact, I liked their comment. They thought I was a very young and good-looking girl and that made me feel kind of happy!

As I entered my sister-in-law Seethai's house, she welcomed me. I told her, "We are going to conduct the *Poonul* ceremony for Ambi. Your brother said that he has written to you already. I came to Thiruvananthapuram to invite you and Manni. You should plan on coming well in advance and be there with us to help us conduct the ceremony." Her husband was then working with one Uppalam Krishnaiyer in Thiruvananthapuram.

My sister-in-law immediately replied, "Your mother can come and help you out. What do I know? And what status do I have?" This was her usual manner of speaking.

So, I told her, "Manni will never come. She rarely comes to your house in Vadiveeswaram. She doesn't go anywhere since Appa's passing away. And she will definitely not attend auspicious functions."

Despite all my explanations, my sister-in-law kept repeating, "She will come..."

By this time her husband, Natarajan, who was listening to this exchange, could not take it anymore. He said, "If you don't want to go just say so. Why do you have to be so difficult? How many times will you repeat that her mother will come?"

At this point, my sister-in-law said, "How can I not attend my brother's son's *Poonul*?" I told them I will be spending the night at Karamanai and then go to Nager-coil in the morning. They told me it was getting late and asked if I could go on my own to Karamanai. I told them that Natarajan, my brother, will come to take me home. In a while, Natarajan arrived to take me home.

I was thrilled that my sister-in-law's husband had rather firmly put her in her place. She had the habit of not talking back to him and dealing with all his criticism with winsome smiles. I thought at least someone like him was there to control this demoness.

Manni gave me 250 rupees to buy clothes for my husband, Ambi and myself for the *Poonul*, and she told me that my brother Natarajan and sister Krishna would come for the *Poonul*. Meena was at that time somewhere in North India with her daughter. Even if she were here, she would not come. She never attended such functions. She did not even attend the marriages of her siblings despite the loving pressure from everyone. When Meena's three granddaughters got married, she was there in the house but did not come to the marriage hall. Strangely it so happened that she attended my daughter's marriage because she was not aware there was a marriage happening.

Out of the 250 rupees Manni gave me I bought myself a nine-yard silk sari for 25 rupees and gave the rest of the money to Chidamabaram. As promised, my brother Natarajan and sister Krishna came from Thiruvanantha-puram for the *Poonul*. Also present were my sister Kunji from Tirunelveli with her husband Raman. (They hadn't yet had any children.) My sister Krishna was very young. She was only one and a half years older than my oldest daughter Shobha. My family members left soon after the religious ceremonies in the morning. They could have stayed for the party in the evening, but no one from my husband's family invited them. As always I felt I did not have the liberty or right to ask them to stay.

Manni had sent a large stainless steel vessel filled with rice, as was the custom (wealthier people would give silver vessels). She had also sent a silver plate and a silver scoop as gifts. Seethai had bought silk saris from Thiruvananthapuram for the two daughters-in-law (by then two of Chithi's sons, my husband's step brothers, were married), for Chithi, and she had also bought saris for herself and her sister Pappa. However, she did not get anything for my daughter or me. I asked my husband if Seethai had bought those saris at his request or on her own initiative. All that he could say in reply was that she (Seethai) had said that she needed to buy clothes for the family members for the *Poonul* and he had agreed to pay, assuming she knew best about the customs. How odd that not one thing was given to me or my family members who attended the *Poonul*! I asked him how come he did not tell me about Seethai talking to him about the clothes, and he replied that it never occurred to him and that he felt he was talking for both of us.

Similar conversations between us occurred often. Usually I would stay quiet but would feel immensely irritated. I had no opportunity to have a heart to heart conversation with my husband. Even during the days when he was not earning I did not have an opportunity to tell him what was happening at home. He would go to the court with his father and then he would study or read books until midnight, and at times till 2 a.m. Sometimes he would go to the movies with his friends and then his father would comment that he was not responsible and was whiling away his time watching movies. Once he started earning money, he worked even harder day and night. And there was my father-in-law at home and there was very little private time left to speak with my husband. Anyway, on rare occasions, even if I said something, it did not seem to register with him.

Now back again to the *Poonul*. They had made *murukku* and flour sweet balls to be returned with the vessels with rice that women would bring with them for the occasion as was the custom. Many had gifted money for the occasion, and my father-in-law took some money out of it and gave it as his gift. Many clients had brought coconuts, fruits and betel leaves. After the traditional ceremonies were over, in the evening there was a party. The sweets, *vadai* (the salted doughnuts), coffee and tea for the party was brought by the cooks from below and other family members.

Janaki (my husband's step-brother's wife) was particularly active in doing everything. Out of everyone in the family who attended, I remember Janaki the most. She was beautiful and always dressed well. At the time of her wedding her father had said that I was the best looking of all the daughters-in-law.

I used to tell her, "That was at the time of your marriage. I don't look the same now."

She would say, "You look the same. You have not become a grandmother or something. It is only three years since I got married. You look the same. Even my husband has said that Chellammal is more beautiful than you and can also sing very well." That made me very happy but I did not want to acknowledge it.

I had told her, "Nobody in this house including my children care about me or respect me."

She had then said, "My husband, my entire family, and myself have great regard for you. We like you a lot." I remembered this conversation when I saw Janaki. She became busy serving the people who had come for the *Poonul* party. She was dressed very elegantly. Chithi, Paatti and myself were downstairs. I also got busy with greeting and serving the guests.

Some of them had not come for the morning ceremony and had just arrived for the evening party. One of them was Seethai's sister-in-law (husband's sister). She asked me, "Why are you wearing an old sari? This is your son's ceremony. You should be wearing a grand silk sari. Didn't anyone from your in-laws' house get a good sari for you?"

I replied, "I just managed to buy a modest sari with the money my mother gave me."

That was a nine-yard sari. Those days for such functions it was customary to buy a nine-yard sari. This is a sari meant for Brahmin women. Married Brahmin women always wore nine-yard saris in my time. But this changed over time. Now, this habit is almost gone. But older ladies would wear only nine-yard saris when they attended marriages, rituals and other occasions in the family. But a widow did not have to do any of this for she never attended her own children's marriages, any rituals or functions of the family, in any case. It has been so as far as I know. Even if some modern girls invite them to come and take part, they would politely refuse, saying that they did not feel up to it and not to force them. Since the custom has been there for many years, they have imbibed it and accepted it. When I start writing about such things I cannot stop. So let me come back to the *Poonul* function.

In the evening we put *murukku* and the sweet flour balls in the vessels brought by the women and also gave them coconuts and betel leaves and betel nuts, when they took leave. Some of them wanted to see the boy for whom the sacred thread ceremony had been done. I don't remember if Ambi came down or not. Later as she was leaving, Seethai's sister-in-law commented, "This girl is very timid. Now that Chidambaram is earning so much, couldn't she get a nice sari for herself?" Everyone agreed with her. It struck me later that Seethai had not only excluded me, she had also not bought a silk skirt for my daughter, supposedly her favourite niece. Actually, neither had I, and for a long time, I felt bad about it. I had not exercised my rights for so long that I never thought I had the right to spend my husband's money. Even if I had taken the liberty with my husband's money and bought her a silk skirt, I would have had to listen to my father-in-law's venomous rants about how irresponsible I was, money did not grow on trees, and how my husband was under my thumb, etc.

So the reality was that I couldn't have even the small things I wanted. For example, 40 days after I had delivered Kumar, I realised I had only two saris. Both were old and torn. I said to my husband, "I have no saris to wear and I would like to buy a couple of simple saris."

He said, "What stops you?"

I told him, "Your father will make some nasty comments."

"There is nothing I can do about it," he answered.

"Even though you are doing well financially, I am forced to live in the same old way. You don't stand up for me and you act like it doesn't matter to you. Your brothers' wives all have a trunk full of saris. They are free to do whatever they want. I wish you had taken a job in a different town and moved."

He replied, "I probably would not be making this much money if we had moved."

"Whatever you earn is of no use to my children or me. Many have moved to places like Madras, Bombay and Calcutta and keep their wives and children happy. They fully accept what their wives tell them. Their wives have full freedom; they live comfortably within their means. Your brothers' wives live such lives. Whatever good things I have or not, I certainly get an earful from everyone every day…"

He replied, "All I can do now is give you money. You should go and buy what you want." He then went to bed.

Coming back to the *Poonul* function, after everything was over I went upstairs around 10 p.m. My husband, his sisters, and his younger brother's wife, Janaki, were all looking at the gifts. Nobody noticed me except my husband. He asked, "Did you just come up?" I replied, "Yes."

He then said, "Come see all these silver vessels that have been gifted."

I said, "I can see them tomorrow."

He said, "Why do you sound so disinterested?"

I replied, "The baby is sleeping downstairs and I am going down to be with him."

We did not have a good cot at that time. We had a bed, which was given to me during my nuptials. I have mentioned it earlier. I have also mentioned that it was too small for two people to sleep in. It was a nice bed, beautifully upholstered. It had been placed in one corner in the upstairs hall. They had spread a large, thickly woven carpet-like fabric on the floor, and a few relatives from my husband's family were sleeping on that. Most women came and slept on that carpet. My sisters-in-law, Seethai and Pappa, had gone to sleep in Seethai's house in the next street. I am not sure what sleeping arrangements were made for the men; maybe they were in a lodge or the office building across the street or in Seethai's house. I am sticking to writing down only what I completely remember. I don't remember where exactly Chidambaram slept. Before leaving to go downstairs I did tell my husband what was bothering me deeply.

"Everyone from your family is here upstairs. How come you did not care about your wife—the *Poonul* boy's mother—not being present? Nowhere else can this happen."

He replied, "It is getting late. Your complaints can wait till tomorrow. Everybody is asleep. I have to sleep. I have to be up early to study the case so that I can be ready for the court." Somebody had made a bed for him in one corner by spreading a thin carpet and placing a pillow on it. The upstairs was a pretty large area. The women were sleeping soundly.

With a heavy heart, I went downstairs and lay down near my baby boy. I could not sleep. There was a place in that large carpet for me, but I came down for the sake of the child. That large carpet-like spread was a gift that someone had given at the time of Seethai's son Thandu's wedding. She had given it to her parental home thinking it would be useful during functions when many visitors came. It was particularly useful for women. It was almost early morning when I dozed off to sleep. I woke up when my little boy began to cry (he rarely cried). As I stepped into the kitchen, the women who were at work there were talking about me. My sisters-in-law were not there.

Paatti was telling Chithi, "It is her son's *Poonul* that has been celebrated and she is sleeping. She is so irresponsible." Others concurred with her.

Then Chithi said to Chindalu Athai (my father-in-law's sister), "My daughters-in-law are so active. And it is her son's function. As the host she should be up early and getting things done…" (Please note: This is a family that supposedly does not distinguish among its different members. And here Chithi was saying "My daughters-in-law".)

At this point, I think Chindalu Athai saw me and she quickly added, "She is quite young and was probably tired after a day's work during the *Poonul* and must have been exhausted. After all, we are all here and we can help." No one liked what she said.

Chithi and Paatti did not like her reply at all. Paatti shot back, "How can any one say she is young? At her age, my daughter (referring to Chithi) was handling the responsibility of being both a mother and a stepmother."

"That is okay," said Chindalu Athai.

As I listened to this exchange, I asked, "Do you want me to grind for the *kozhambu*?"

Paatti said, "That is not necessary anymore, go and have your bath."

After my bath, I had some coffee. Both the sisters-in-law had come over with their husbands. Not quite sure if Thandu had also come. The men along with two family priests sat down in the main hall for lunch. Banana leaves were spread to serve lunch. I helped with serving lunch. Finally, all of us women sat down to eat. I told them I would serve myself and eat, but no one would listen. Since my stomach was upset I could not relish what I was eating. After serving us, Chindalu Athai and Paatti had their lunch.

After the *Poonul*, all of my husband's brothers and their wives left. Pappa, my sister-in-law from Bombay, stayed back with her daughter for a while. I had always wanted to see Bombay and I badly needed to be away from this house for a while. So, I took permission from my husband and left with Pappa—although she had not extended an invitation to me—taking my baby Kumar with me. At that time, I believe my daughter Shobha was staying with Seethai in Thiruvananthapuram and was doing her intermediate course in the college. Around that time, they had added a new class of train compartment called Inter Class. This was more comfortable than the regular economy third class compartment. Pappa had a free pass for the train since her husband worked for the railways. I had to buy a ticket for myself. In those days we had to first get to Madras before going to Bombay. Everyone in the house except my husband disapproved of my trip. I was so eagerly looking forward to seeing Bombay that I could not care less about their comments and ignored them completely.

In the train, Kumar, my year-old baby, got fever and I was overcome with worry. I made baby food and slowly fed him throughout the trip as I prayed.

During the night Pappa woke up and said, "The baby is sleeping, why don't you just rest?"

I replied, "I don't want to lie down. I cannot sleep anyway. Only when his fever goes can I relax."

She said, "It is 2 a.m. and we will reach Madras soon. We can see a doctor right away then and everything will be okay." After saying this, she went back to sleep. Her 14-year-old daughter was also fast asleep.

As soon as we reached Madras my husband's brother Vaidyanathan had his regular physician visit and examine the baby. The doctor prescribed some medicine and Kumar recovered within a day. I was so relieved. I remember there was a family friend visiting Vaidyanathan's place at that time. He commented, "Why is Chellammal taking this small baby and going to Bombay?" Pappa agreed and said she felt the same, but had not said it since she did not want it misinterpreted as me not being welcome. For a moment I thought I will just go back home, even though that in itself would be a major undertaking if I had to do it on my own. I told myself that the baby is now okay; I would rather go to Bombay than go back to that house in Vadiveeswaram.

That night we left by Bombay Mail and spent two nights on the train. Since it was a new trip and route for me, I was not bored. The train arrived at Dadar early in the morning. We took a taxi to the house in Matunga. The houses in Bombay were small, just one room and a kitchen. All the houses were in a row facing one another. The kitchen was very conveniently designed with a lot of storage space. Nothing needed to be piled up on the kitchen floor. There was running water all the time in the kitchen. Pappa kept the place very clean. They had to share common toilets and bathrooms with other apartments. Pappa would send me for sightseeing around 11 a.m., after having a meal. We would all get up early to have our baths. Pappa's husband, Srinivasan, and his neighbour who was a friend would take me out, while Pappa would take care of the baby. We went by bus or by the local train. We visited popular spots like Malabar Hill, the museum,[13] Mahalaxmi Temple, Juhu Beach, etc. Pappa took me to Gandhi Market, where I bought a georgette sari, a dress for my girl, and a toy for the baby. We also visited a few friends and relatives. When I returned from sightseeing at the end of the day, my baby boy was always awake and waiting for me. Pappa was a good cook. For some reason, she never smiled and I had the feeling that she really did not like me being there.

Finally, she found an escort for me to return home. This was a young man who was travelling to Tirunelveli. Those days the train only went up to Tirunelveli. From there one had to take a bus to Nagercoil. Chidambaram had come with a taxi to pick me up at the Tirunelveli bus station since we did not have a car then. As soon as we reached home, my son seemed thrilled to be back in the large house and started running around with joy. I forgot to mention that one could not travel from Bombay to

---

[13] Chellammal was probably referring to the Prince of Wales Museum (now Chhatrapati Shivaji Maharaj Vastu Sangrahalaya) that was easily accessible by bus from Matunga.

Nagercoil directly those days. One had to come to Madras and then go to Nagercoil. Thanu stayed in Abhiramapuram and Vaidyanathan and his wife, Valli, lived in the Luz area with their child Lalitha. Lalitha was seven months older than Kumar. She was an active child all the time running around. She would keep pinching Kumar. Kumar was a docile child. He never gave any trouble where food was concerned.

After I got back home, everyone started their usual grumbling in a matter of days. On the *Poonul* day, it had become late at night and I could not complete my conversation with Chidambaram. I could not talk to him about what had been left unsaid the next day either. Not just that, till I left for Bombay the opportunity to speak to him never arose. The night I returned I continued that incomplete conversation with him.

I once again brought up my grievance with my husband and asked him, "How come when all your family was gathered after the *Poonul,* you did not bother to notice the fact I was not around and that nobody asked me to join in looking at the gifts? Nowhere else can this happen. It does not matter that no one else cared. How come you didn't? That is what makes me sad."

He replied, "It was your son's *Poonul.* You should have taken the initiative and should have joined me in welcoming and taking care of everyone. The others did everything with so much responsibility."

I said, "I still don't think it was right that you ignored me. It means you really don't care enough. No husband who loves his wife would behave in that fashion... You never take my side and talk on my behalf. Every day I wake up wondering what kind of insults I have to put up with. Does anyone else in this house have to face such a painful situation? If only you can make up your mind, you can provide me with a life of freedom and happiness like the lives your sisters and sisters-in-law enjoy. We may quarrel. But that is a different matter. I have told you many times. But you say you can't leave Anna alone and come. I don't think I can stay in this house anymore. Let me suggest something. Please look for a house in Nagercoil village and settle us there. I will stay there with my child. You can visit us whenever possible. There is one more thing. You must give half of what you earn." I spoke at one go, not pausing to take a breath.

His reply was short. He asked, "Is that all? Or do you have more to say?"

"If I remember everything it would all come pouring out one after the other. I have hardly found any time when you are free so that I can speak to you. You wake up at 6 a.m., have your coffee and finish the rest of the work, then take a bath, and immediately go to your office across. When you come back at 10 a.m., it is to eat and then you go to court, coming back only at 5 p.m...." (Sometimes he also went to the courts at Thakkalai and Kuzhithurai. So long as his father was alive, he never came home for the afternoon tiffin. He would have *vadai* or *dosai* and coffee at the old Pothi Hotel next to the court. This was a habit from my father-in-law's time.)

I continued, "You then go out for a walk and come back when it is almost dark. At 8 p.m., you eat dinner and disappear back into your office before 9 p.m. You finally come home only by eleven or even later at midnight.

You have your own keys to get in, so I don't even have to bother opening the door for you. When do I have time to tell you anything? You don't know anything about what is happening at home. Even if you come to know, you will not care to question people on my behalf. So find me a house. I would be better off living by myself with the baby." I poured my heart out to him.

"Don't be stupid, what you are saying is not practical. You just should not pay attention to what anyone says. Get yourself whatever you want. Don't bother about what Anna says," he replied.

"I knew this is how you would respond. That is why I don't tell you anything."

There was also another reason why I did not always talk to him this way. He would get worked up and say, "Listening to you makes my blood pressure go up. It is going to make me bleed and die." I wonder even now if he just said that to frighten me. This man would never know what I have to endure in this house, and I don't have the guts to commit suicide. It looks like there is going to be no release from this hell. Every morning I get up thinking who is going to bad-mouth me today. Who else in this house goes through this fate? All kinds of thoughts ran through my mind.

One day I came back home after watching a popular movie *Apoorva Sagotharargal* (in which Bhanumathi and M.K. Radha acted) for the second time. It was a very popular film of those days. I don't remember if I took my children. I had only two children, a boy and a girl, at that time. The next morning, it was 7 a.m. when I came down. My father-in-law seemed to be waiting for me in the front room near the staircase. He started yelling, "Who do you think you are? How dare you go and watch a movie twice? You can get away with anything because you are arrogant that your husband is making good money; so you will sleep till 7 a.m. and the others have to serve you!" He continued on his rant. I was hurting inside but I did not say anything, as usual.

That movie was so popular in those days. And my friend Gyanambal had said to me, "Everyone is going to see the movie a second time. Come with us." I had already wanted to go, so I did not need much convincing. When I came back late at night, I was scared of what my father-in-law would say. And Chithi grumbled as she opened the door for me. As I expected, my father-in-law gave me a tongue lashing the next morning. And I stood there tongue-tied.

Then I went about doing my daily chores. My husband asked me later, "What did Anna say about you going to the movies?"

I replied, "He thinks I am wasting your hard-earned money. When you were not earning anything I lived like a beggar. When you are doing so well, why should my children and I continue to live like that? Why don't you put in a word that I have equal rights to your money and that he shouldn't interfere in such silly matters? Why don't you speak to that father of yours?"

He remonstrated, "I have told you many times. Just ignore him and do what you have to do. You can also talk back and give him a suitable reply. Besides that, I cannot do anything else. And do not call him names."

I said, "Your sister uses such language when she speaks of my father."

He replied, "You are better than that. If you have to follow someone follow their good behaviour, not their nastiness. You are really a good woman. You should behave properly. That is all I can say. I really want to keep you and our children happy."

I said, "It is not enough to have just good intentions. There will only be trouble so long as we are here. Even if you do not intercede on my behalf, you should at least question them when they mistreat me. I feel I will have freedom only in death but I don't have the courage to take my own life. Besides, I have this small baby. The other children are all grown up."

He then said, "Don't be stupid. Between you and Anna I am going to be driven to my death."

I said, "Please don't say such things. That is the reason I do not confide in you. Besides, you have no time for me. Even on Sundays, you spend the whole day in the office. For merely watching a movie a second time your father questioned me as if he was questioning a criminal in court. And it was a matter of just a quarter of a rupee…"

(In those days in the local Pioneer theatre a balcony ticket for women just cost 4 annas, a quarter of a rupee. When women were being degraded all over, the theatre owner had made this arrangement for women to honour them and respect them. The balcony was divided into two parts, for women and men, with a screen in between. One entire section was for women and the cost was, as I said, just 4 annas. The other section was for men. In the men's section, both men and women could sit, and usually, women came with their husbands. Once Chidambaram took me to that section when he went to watch a movie with two of his friends because one of his friends insisted he brings his wife. I don't think the children were born then.)

I continued to vent out my feelings. "For spending this paltry amount your father made it seem like I had spent thousands of rupees and you could hear him from upstairs. You could have easily told him that he should not bother me for such insignificant matters. You should tell him that he should not be concerned with how much you spend and that your wife has full ownership of everything you earn, and that you didn't get her or your children anything for 12 years as you were not earning any money and that was the main reason you didn't want to spend your father's money on your family in the past. You must say that to your father!" I insisted.

Once again he said, "I can never talk like that to Anna. Ignore Anna. You should spend money on whatever you want..."

I was hoping that someday he would stand up on my behalf, even though I never believed it would really happen. There was no point in talking to him. I have to live all my life with these people. I almost felt that he did not love me. If he did, he should have taken cognizance of what was happening at home. I was not used to making a scene. He may have even thought that he could easily console me and get things done his way.

At times I wished I had finished high school. I could have found a job. I could have found a way for my livelihood. I could have found freedom from this hell. All I ended up learning was cooking.

In Karamanai, my hometown, there was this lady Laxmi who could be hired to make the traditional snacks for marriages. She usually hired some helpers. When they worked, they were given food, coffee, etc. She was popular and would be hired for functions in other towns. Once, when I was visiting my family home, I met her and (in my desperation to be independent) I suggested that I work for her. She was very upset and started yelling. Manni and sister came out of the kitchen wondering what was going on. Laxmi then said, "Look at what your daughter is saying. She wants to work with me. She is married into a wealthy family. She shouldn't talk this way."

"She was wrong but she is desperate. She has no freedom in that house. They treat her like a worm. She may seem talkative when she visits her birth home but out there, in her in-laws' place, she rarely opens her mouth. Also, her husband does not interfere or help when her in-laws abuse her verbally. At one time her husband was not earning any money and would use that as a reason to be frugal, but now even though he makes good money, her father-in-law makes a big fuss about minor expenses. Overall, she is very unhappy in that house. She is not even able to buy things for her children. Her husband is educated. Like everyone else, we thought he would get a job and move out of town but that never happened," Manni told her.

Laxmi replied, "Your daughter will never make it if she is so timid. Let her husband take good care of his father, but he has a duty to take care of his wife too since she is totally dependent on him. He could move out to a house nearby with his wife and the little one. (My two older children were studying out of town by then.) He can then easily also care for his father."

I said, "He will never do anything like that."

As she was leaving, Laxmi said to me, "It is probably your fate. Anyway, don't do anything stupid, good times will come."

The day after this my husband had come to take me. Manni had made flour powder made of chickpea and sugar and kept it ready. When my husband had written that he may come in a week to take me she had got it all ready. She poured hot ghee and made sweet balls. I think he had come in a client's car. I remember going by car. Those days I used to take the bus to go to my parental home. Thakkalay and Kuzhithurai are villages close to Nagercoil. Kuzhithurai was 32 km away. Frequently, he had to go for cases in Thakkalay and Kuzhithurai, so he decided to buy a car. I really think he used the case travel as an excuse to buy the car; otherwise, his father would have made a big fuss. My husband's income was soon steadily increasing, and he had always wanted to get a car. If I used the car to go to the centre of the town (a very short distance), my father-in-law and sister-in-law would make disapproving comments. They would say the car was meant for official trips only. This would irritate me. Where else can you see such nonsense... It seemed very unfair. I would feel so angry. I would boil inwardly at this injustice. I would wish I could throw big stones on their heads. But as usual, I would keep quiet.

I never had support from my children either. By the time the car was bought, the two older children had grown up but they did not have the love or respect for me as a mother. Listening to all the derisive comments of my sisters-in-law, I believe they felt I was stupid. My daughter Shobha called my sister-in-law Amma (mother), while she used to call me by my name. Later she must have thought about it and started calling me Amma. In Karamanai, my folks noticed her calling me by name and were surprised. More than any of these things, what bothered me most was that my husband did not care or support me.

Whatever happens, time cannot be stopped. Father-in-law developed a wound in his back. He also had diabetes. His son (my husband) gave him his daily insulin injections and dressed his wound daily. He became bedridden and had to use a bedpan. Chithi had to clean his clothes. As I have said before, in those days men who lost their wives married again almost immediately. It did not matter if the man was old or had many children; there were enough young women from poor families available for those men. Most of those women were illiterate. Once in a while when a man would object to remarrying, his family would force him. They would argue that he needed someone to care for him as he got old and sick. No one bothered about the fate of women. It was ordained that women were there just to serve the man.

So it was Chithi's turn to serve her husband, who was bedridden for about six months. Until the end, his mind was sharp. He was well cared for by his wife and eldest son (my husband). Suddenly he developed a high fever. The temperature kept increasing and went beyond what a thermometer could measure. The son was informed and by the time he brought the doctor, father-in-law had lost consciousness. Within a short while he passed away with his son at his bedside. He was 72 when he died. Seethai had arrived before he got fever. Everything was done according to customs. Only a year after his death, after the annual rituals for the departed were done, Chithi and Paatti left for Thiruvananthapuram to live with Chithi's second son Ganapathi.

Ganapathi worked in the Reserve Bank. His wife Janaki was afflicted with polio and was bedridden. She had a heart operation done at Vellore. The Vellore Hospital had a very good reputation but it was not as good as it is today, at that time. Janaki died after the operation. Ganapathi was deeply depressed after her death. Janaki was beautiful and a very smart person. She was a good cook. They had a daughter and a son, and she took good care of them. She also did everything that a wife was supposed to do. His second wife, Nithya, was also a beautiful woman. She was a good homemaker and took good care of Ganapathi too. Ganapathi is no more now. He was only 32 when he got married a second time. All Chithi's sons died one after the other. Chithi has been gone a long time too. Fortunately, she did not have to experience the loss of her sons. Chithi always used to say that she and Seethai were the same age. Maybe she had this unvoiced feeling that she was marrying someone her father's age. The second wives could not be as free as the first wives. It was only after Chithi got her own daughters-in-law that she could defy Seethai in some ways.

Seethai, however, did manage to do a final drama before my father-in-law breathed his last. When father-in-law had become bedridden, Chithi's son Neelakantan's wife was six or seven months pregnant. They always perform the *Seemantham*, a ceremony conducted for the first pregnancy of the woman in her husband's house. Seethai said that since my father-in-law's condition was bad, there was no need for a grand function and invite a lot of people; that it can be a simple one with just the family and the family priest conducting the rituals.

After Seethai left, Neelakantan said, "I feel like inviting everyone and properly conducting the *Seemantham*."

Chithi also said, "That is the way it should be done. We have not invited Neelakantan's in-laws and given them a festive meal. We can invite them now on this occasion."

"Of course, we will celebrate it grandly. Nothing will happen to Anna. Give me a list of the things you need for the *Seemantham*. I will give you the money. You don't have to worry," said Chithi's stepson, my husband. The preparations then started in earnest. Echiatha Anna, my father-in-law's brother, provided all the needed help.

I think Chithi went personally to invite Seethai. She was her daughter after all. Chithi always used to refer to her stepdaughter as a daughter; maybe because she was her husband's daughter. On the day of the *Seemantham*, Gomathi's (Neelakantan's wife) parents and many other relatives came for the function. They performed the *Valaikaappu*, the bangle ceremony, early in the morning. The girl's family had to perform that ceremony. Normally it was performed in the fifth month of pregnancy. The giving of many gifts was associated with the ceremony, including food gifts. The important one was preparation with different kinds of lentils fried and mixed with some other ingredients added to the mixture that was specially done for this occasion. It was a time-consuming and tiring job to prepare this. The bangle ceremony was, as I have said, the responsibility of the girl's family. In earlier days it was done at the girl's parental home and often done simply. From Gomathi's house, they had brought the mixture along with milk sweet, *murukku* and many other savouries. After the ceremony everyone had their morning tiffin. The *Seemantham* ceremony began around 10 or 11 a.m. Everyone began to worry that Seethai had not turned up for the function. Chithi told Pappa to somehow bring Seethai. Pappa brought her, almost dragging her. There was a lot of crying. Pappa pleaded with her to stop, but Seethai would not listen to anyone and was (inconsolable).

****

Made in the USA
Monee, IL
08 July 2026

56691872R00111